Retraining

Retraining

TEACHING NEW SKILLS TO
PREVIOUSLY TRAINED HORSES

SHARON B. SMITH

HOWELL BOOK HOUSE

NEW YORK

The information given in this book is provided for the purpose of education and to give as complete a picture as possible. The reader, even if experienced in the handling of horses, should exercise extreme care in all circumstances.

All photographs by the author

Howell Book House
A Simon & Schuster Macmillan Company
1633 Broadway
New York, NY 10019

MACMILLAN is a registered trademark of Macmillan, Inc.

Library of Congress Cataloging-in-Publication Data
Smith, Sharon B.
    Retraining: teaching new skills to previously trained horses /
Sharon B. Smith
        p. cm.
    Includes index.
    ISBN 0-87605-285-5
    1. Horses—Training. 2. Horsemanship. I. Title.
SF287.S55   1998
636.1'0888—dc21   97-35212
                                                                              CIP

BOOK DESIGN BY KEVIN HANEK

Manufactured in the United States of America

10   9   8   7   6   5   4   3   2   1

Contents

PART ONE

Preparing to Retrain

CHAPTER ONE

Why Retrain?

THOSE OF US WHO LOVE HORSES usually begin to dream about training them within a few weeks of discovering our affection. Although we might read training books by the dozen, the dream usually remains just that. Training is a long, difficult process that requires more skill, time, and determination than most people have. We do, however, tend to remember the books we read and wish that we could train by following their instructions.

One of the reasons most of us remain wishers rather than doers is a premise that pervades books, training barns, and backyard pastures alike: the assumption that you have to start from the beginning, with an unbroken young horse, in order to end up with an animal that is properly trained for his sport or use. The extent to which experts acknowledge reality is limited to noting that you might occasionally acquire a horse that needs a little finishing or one that might have a few vices which must be eliminated.

The real world is an entirely different place. Very few of us are ever faced with a blank-page horse, one that has never been taught anything by anyone. If the horse you already own or are thinking about buying is one of the vast majority of horses that somebody else got to first, you are hardly alone.

It's not that you don't want a horse that already knows exactly what you expect it to do. A horse well trained for his work represents cooperation between man and nature at its best. The horse knows what to do, and his body helps him do it. Anyone who acquires a horse hopes and intends to reach this point.

People with money and luck reach this point quickly, having obtained a horse that somebody else trained well for the exact purpose they have in mind. Instant gratification is a very enjoyable concept, with horses as with anything else.

Others, who have the time and skill, train their own horses. They can devote years to turning a young horse into a usable adult animal. The gratification may be delayed, but it usually arrives.

Most of us don't fit into either of these categories, lacking either money, skill, time, or all three, so we acquire a horse that somebody else has trained. Most likely, the original trainer didn't share our precise goals, and we have a horse that has to be fixed.

We all know it can be done. After all, almost everybody who has ever bought an adult horse has done at least a little fixing, probably begrudging the time involved and wishing for a bank account that would have allowed the purchase of a perfect horse to begin with. But retraining is more than a little fixing.

This handsome young Standardbred will be looking for a new career once he's no longer competitive on the racetrack.

Nevertheless, it is far from being something to dread and can even be better than shopping exclusively among made horses in your own equine sport. There are always many more adult horses than untrained young ones on the market. This statement is supported by the fact that the average horse's life expectancy now exceeds twenty years. Even if the age of adulthood is conservatively set at five years, there will be at least three times as many full-grown horses as young ones. Most of these mature horses will have been trained for something specific, but chances are that it will be an equine discipline other than yours (unless yours is simple leisure riding).

These numbers alone make it likely that you will acquire (or at least consider taking on) a previously trained horse at some point in your equine career. The same numbers present you with the opportunity to find a very good horse—possibly a better one than you might find if you only look among untrained young animals and expensive, well-trained horses already doing the kind of work you want.

These horses become available for sale or adoption for different reasons, some of which require the buyer to devote a great deal of care and attention to the horse. Other reasons for availability are more benign, and buyers looking for good prospects can be a little less guarded. Here's a look at some examples from both categories.

WHY HORSES BECOME AVAILABLE

LOSS OF INTEREST

At the companion-horse or casual-riding level, thousands of animals become available each year simply because their owners lose interest in keeping them. There are dozens of reasons people give up good horses that serve them well: a child goes off to college, a family moves to a home that lacks the space needed to maintain a horse, or the board bills become too difficult to pay.

This is an excellent category in which to search for a retraining prospect. While there are exceptions, horses in this group tend to be sound, good-natured, and amenable to retraining. Some have acquired vices and many more need special work to get them back into shape for regular use, but if the owner's loss of interest is the only reason for their availability, they are good candidates for retraining.

OUTGROWN HORSES

Horses are also offered for sale because their riders have outgrown them—in size, ambition, or both. A horse bought because, at the time, he was the proper size for a child or young teenager will be too small within a few years of the purchase. Thousands of under-16-hand horses and ponies come onto the market each year for this reason.

Outgrown horses and ponies provide some of the best retraining prospects. Most of them find homes with a smaller person in the same sport or usage category. But the animals that are being discarded because they don't live up to their young rider's expectations might be

When Emma outgrows her pony, he can be retrained to drive.

good candidates for a career change. For example, a poor-to-average, large hunter pony may have great potential as a Western pleasure horse. A Shetland that scarcely tolerated his child rider may prove to be an outstanding driving pony for an adult.

Occasionally the horse outgrows the rider. A young horse bought for a young rider may become bigger than expected. This is uncommon, since young, growing horses are rarely matched with children. A more likely scenario sees a young horse develop in a way that proves to be unsuitable for his sport. A well-conformed stock-horse yearling may grow up to have a high head, long back, and light hindquarters—making him a poor Western sport prospect but a likely driving horse.

LACK OF TALENT

Horses are often sold because they lack the talent for their original intended use. Some of them are outgrown horses and simply drop down to a lower level within their original sports. But others make up a category of their own.

Horses bred specifically for highly specialized sports often enjoy very little latitude in performance. With a Thoroughbred racehorse, three seconds to the mile is the difference between a champion and one that can barely earn his keep. A gaited horse that can't quite manage his breed's distinctive gaits will not be able to compete, regardless of how superb he may be in every other way. A cutting horse that lacks cow sense will almost never successfully cut out a steer.

Sometimes conformation characteristics make particular movements difficult. For example, a roping horse narrow in the hindquarters will never be able to make the kind of stops required to succeed in his sport. Likewise, these characteristics may prevent a horse from going beyond a certain level in his sport, no matter how willing he is and how well he's been trained. A warmblood with a short neck and a low head is never going to get the shape required for top-level dressage. A gaudy pinto may never receive the respect from hunter judges that he may deserve. But each may be able to go further in a sport that suits his conformation and appearance. Both the low-headed warmblood and the pinto will draw admiring glances in a Western pleasure class.

Callie wasn't much of a racehorse, but she's
already on her way to becoming a hunter-jumper
show horse.

LACK OF SOUNDNESS

In a perfect world, you would never even consider acquiring a horse with soundness problems. But the world is no more perfect than any of the horses in it, and soundness will be a consideration whenever you look at a potential equine purchase, whether he is already trained for your sport or not. Many horses become available because they are too unsound for continued use in their own sports.

If you retrain, you may be able to accept more unsoundness than his original owner could. You will certainly be able to accept different kinds of unsoundness, and this flexibility increases the number of horses you can consider.

A horse with even minor navicular disease in the front feet will never be able to stay sound in activities like jumping and racing, which cause concussion to the front hooves. But a mildly navicular horse is generally sound enough for trail riding, driving, reining, dressage, and other nongalloping sports.

A horse with arthritic hocks probably can't progress very far in dressage, and he probably would make a terrible barrel racer. But he can be ridden at most levels of English and Western pleasure, and he can usually be driven successfully.

Because of the potential for back injury, a long-backed horse is considered poorly conformed in most sports. But a tall, long-legged rider who doesn't use a forward seat needs a long-backed horse in order to be comfortable.

THE DIFFICULT HORSE

Some horses become available because they have habits, vices, or general personality traits that make them too difficult for their riders to handle. Whether or not these horses are likely candidates for retraining depends upon the problems and your abilities and willingness to do another level of retraining before you get to train the horse for your sport.

Most bad habits are superficial and can be changed, but some are such a deep part of a particular equine character—particularly in an older horse—that retraining becomes a longer and more difficult task than training a young horse from scratch. Look carefully before choosing a retraining prospect in this category so you can avoid profound problems.

BENEFITS OF BUYING A PREVIOUSLY TRAINED HORSE

PRICE

In addition to enjoying the fact that you will have a larger number of horses to consider, you may find that you can get a better horse for less if you are willing to retrain. This is true for most of the same reasons that lead to increased availability.

Certainly, some of those available horses are unlikely to qualify as bargains. Among these are the outgrown horses, since they often remain in their own sports. An outgrown horse may actually cost a little more than he should, since the owner may need extra money to buy a larger or more skilled animal.

Other nonbargains include horses from sports in which people are so used to paying big money that even a moderately talented animal will cost more than a star performer in a less expensive activity.

You can't judge by the activity itself either. Despite the fact that polo is viewed by many as an upper-crust sport, the best polo pony in the world is worth less than the worst Grand Prix jumper around. The cheapest Thoroughbred at Santa Anita is still worth $20,000. The pricey sports may provide retraining prospects, but they generally don't provide bargains, at least until the horses drop down through the ranks to the lowest level of competition within their original sports.

Some breed organizations also help ensure that less-talented members of their respective breeds have a chance to retain their value. Morgans are now shown in Western pleasure classes, and Quarter Horses can succeed as English-style hunters without leaving their breed shows. People involved with these breeds do find themselves retraining adult horses, but they often do it with a horse that they already own.

Still, many retraining prospects are indeed available with far lower price tags than their quality and potential should command. Horses with conformation characteristics considered incorrect for their breed or sport are likely to be reasonably priced. A light-boned, short draft horse owned by someone who leases teams to pull heavy wagons in parades is likely to be a bargain for somebody looking for a sturdy riding horse. The stock horse with the narrow hindquarters should be reasonably priced and will be perfectly suited to an endurance rider.

Horses being given up by people who can't afford the upkeep may be the best bargains of all. Somebody who wants to stop paying a $300-a-month board bill will probably worry less about the price he gets for the horse than about the day the new owner starts paying that bill. Parents hoping to unload a horse used by a child who has lost interest in it are also probably not looking for a profit.

BETTER PREDICTIONS OF FUTURE SUCCESS

Another reason to choose retraining an adult horse over training a young one is the help he will give you in predicting his eventual skills. You won't know precisely how well he's going to perform his new sport, but you will have a far better idea than you would if your horse were six months old and unbroken.

By choosing a previously trained adult horse, even if the training has been in a different sport than yours, you avoid the risk of his maturing into an unsuitable animal. Yes, you can try to predict what a baby will look like when he's fully grown, but horses don't always grow and mature as you expect them to. A foal with big feet may indeed grow into those feet and become a big horse with appropriate hooves, but he may also grow up to be a small horse with oversized feet.

Previous training will also give you an idea of the horse's willingness and ability to be trained. Although it is often said that there are no bad horses, only bad trainers, some horses just don't seem to learn as well as others. All horses don't have the same respect for human beings, willingness to cooperate with them, or desire to please them. Whatever problem a particular horse has, you may be able to learn about it before acquiring him, provided that he has already been trained for something.

QUICK TURNAROUND

A previously trained adult horse will be usable far sooner than will an untrained young horse. Basic retraining can be so quick that a horse can often be used in his new activity within hours of being introduced to it.

Obviously thorough training takes much longer, but many categories provide remarkably rapid turnaround. Harness horses that have been never ridden will often carry riders after an hour or so of preparation.

The switch from English to Western can be instantaneous if the rider is careful to give double cues right from the start. Other projects have different time requirements, but one fact is true of all categories—you will have a horse to use much sooner than if your horse were an untrained young animal.

Basic horse training is almost always the same regardless of the sport, and this means that retrainers can essentially skip weeks, even months, of work. As you will see, it is wise to go back over the early steps, even if briefly, to get the horse back into a learning mode, but a well-trained horse will remember much of what he has already learned.

CHAPTER TWO

Locating the Retraining Prospect

ROSPECTS FOR RETRAINING COME FROM THE same sources as other horses, but, since some provide better retraining prospects than others, locating a good one requires that you look at some of those sources more carefully than you might otherwise. You will also examine the prospects from a slightly different viewpoint.

Of course, some characteristics are desirable whether you're searching for an untrained yearling, a made horse, or a retraining prospect. You want a horse in good health, sound enough to do the work you intend him to perform, and willing to accept human direction.

Since you will be planning to commit less time and money to training, you can be more flexible and less demanding in your search for an older horse. A mistake won't be so costly. You will be able to choose from a far larger pool of potential purchases. Still, start your search with any of the traditional sources for available horses.

BREEDERS

A breeding farm that specializes in a particular sport or breed is unquestionably the best source for untrained young horses, but it may also be a good source for made horses, particularly if it sends colts out to compete. Although a breeding farm will initially appear to be an unlikely source for retraining prospects (since its older horses will consist only of animals that somebody thought might be good enough to breed), you will find that they offer very promising and very skilled horses. An active farm might train a dozen colts in its sport, hoping to find just one good enough to later stand at stud. The eleven others, as well trained and perhaps almost as good, will eventually be available for purchase.

Most important to you will be the culls. The larger and more professional the farm, the more culls each year. Most breeding-farm culls are broodmares, although you will find the occasional stallion removed from the breeding ranks. Culls are breeding animals that have failed to live up to expectations, either by proving barren or sterile, or by producing poor offspring.

An otherwise healthy mare that didn't work out as a broodmare will be a tremendous bargain and is an excellent candidate for retraining. Most of them will have been well fed, carefully handled, vaccinated, wormed, and generally well treated. In the racing breeds, mares that produce slow babies can be identified after four or five seasons of breeding and may be culled by the age of ten. In other breeds, the mares may be a little older. In either case, the mare may be too old to return to her original sport, making her an ideal prospect for retraining.

Barren mares are identified more quickly. Unless the mare is a Kentucky Derby winner like Genuine Risk, she won't be given more than two or three seasons to prove fertile. You will also find young retraining prospects in this group.

Sometimes, mares that have produced adequate but not outstanding offspring are no longer bred after their mid-teens. These mares have another ten years of moderate use ahead of them and may be good prospects as well.

Breeding farms sometimes sell culls in dispersal auctions, in breeding-stock auctions, through classified ads, and through trainers or dealers. Additionally, you may call a farm and say that you are in the market for a moderately priced barren mare to retrain. Most farm owners and managers really do want good homes for their rejects and will match you with a suitable animal if they can.

Although there certainly are exceptions, the average stallion is not a good prospect for retraining. Most stallions require special housing and handling, and many boarding stables refuse to accept them. Even on your own property, you may find your training time taken up with securing fences and hiding nearby mares.

While their sex does not affect their intellectual capacity, many older stallions are so easily distracted and so used to getting their own way that they are not inclined to concentrate on learning new skills. Male horses can be gelded at any age, although the surgery is slightly more dangerous for a grown horse. If you are prepared to deal with either handling problems or the prospect of surgery, consider a culled stallion as a retraining project (see Chapter Twelve).

AUCTIONS

Auctions can be dangerous places for horse buyers. The danger lies not in the possibility that you might scratch your nose and accidentally make the winning bid on a million-dollar horse. Auctioneers know the difference between a bid and a scratch on the nose, and they are not going to sell a horse to somebody who can't pay for it.

The real danger comes on two fronts. One is the possibility that you might get caught up in the excitement and competition of the moment. In a fit of competitive fire, you may bid more than you want to pay for a particular horse. That problem is easily prevented by setting a maximum limit on each horse that interests you and refusing to go above it, no matter what.

The second problem is much more difficult to overcome. Most auctions give you very little opportunity to examine, test, and assess the horses. Policies of auction companies vary widely, and some are much more generous than others. Almost all will let you look at the horses during a preview period before the auction begins. Many will have the horses led at the walk and trot so that you can assess soundness. Some will allow you to try out a trained horse, although you will probably have to bring your own tack.

You are always allowed to bring a veterinarian or other expert along to advise you. They may not be permitted to draw blood or make tests, but they can examine the horse.

Some auction companies will even have X rays available (or permit you to have your own done), identify cribbers, and verify parentage or parents' produce records. Furthermore, if their information proves inaccurate later on, they will take the horse back. However, they never guarantee performance ability and usually won't guarantee soundness beyond what is apparent at the time of the auction. If your purchase breaks down a month after the auction, don't count on return privileges.

Before you consider bidding on a horse at an auction, request a written copy of auction policy so you know about payment requirements, guarantees, and inspection procedures. If it's an auction of registered horses, a catalog should tell you something about the history of the horse, and you may be able to identify a good but barren mare or a performance horse that didn't quite perform at a high enough level.

Once you've narrowed down the possibilities, inspect and try the horse to the extent you can. Set your limit and bid. You may get a very good horse at a bargain price.

DEALERS

Although horse dealers sell to one person at a time, certain similarities exist between dealers and auctioneers. As with auction houses, each dealer will have a different policy about examinations, tryouts, and guarantees. In general, they are more generous and flexible than auction houses in permitting a buyer to learn about a horse.

Dealers who are inclined to be dishonest have a better opportunity than auctioneers to exaggerate facts or hide problems. They have more time to spend with you and can spend that time convincing you to buy a horse.

Most dealers are basically honest and will not tell you something that is absolutely untrue about a horse. Only a few will go out of their

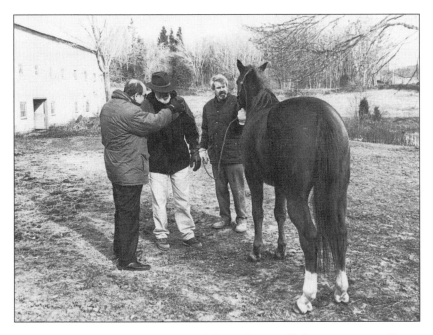

Although dealers and brokers can help you locate a likely prospect, you still need to study the horse carefully.

way to point out physical flaws or characteristics that make a horse unsuitable for you, as most of them are reluctant to give you a reason to look elsewhere.

Keep in mind that you can put into a sales agreement anything that you can get the dealer to agree to. If you are unsure about a horse's suitability, you can ask for a return clause. The dealer may refuse (if he's adamantly opposed, that will give you an idea of his confidence in the quality of his horse), or he may propose terms of his own.

One precaution should always be followed with horse dealers, especially if you have any doubts about his or her horses: Don't agree to buy any horse the first time you see it, particularly if the dealer knew you were coming and prepared the horse for you. Come back another day when you aren't expected. A less-than-honest dealer can give an unsound horse painkillers or a difficult one tranquilizers. You are more likely to see the real horse if you're not expected.

BROKERS

Brokers are dealers operating at a different—often higher—level. With many of them, horse brokerage is a sideline. They may be trainers selling horses that they have trained for clients or breeding-farm managers selling off mares or performance horses for other clients. They may be competitive riders unloading horses that didn't work out for them, or they may be boarding-stable operators or riding instructors helping out students or boarders.

For several reasons, a broker can be the ideal source for a good retraining prospect. Most are horse professionals, so they will have a good idea of what you need and how well their horses match your requirements. They also have reputations to maintain, so they tend to be less likely to try to hide undesirable aspects of a particular horse.

Since most brokers don't make their entire livings selling horses, they may be more generous than other sellers in referring you elsewhere if need be. Some trainers or stable operators, as a favor to a good client, don't even take a fee for arranging a sale.

The most difficult part of buying from brokers is locating them. Some do advertise themselves as brokers, but most sell individual horses in the same way owners do—through private sales.

CLASSIFIED ADS

Of the hundreds and thousands of horses that change hands each year, most are sold by nonprofessionals—sometimes with help from an expert and sometimes not. Unless these horses are sold between friends, they will probably appear in classified ads at some point during their time on the market.

A horse specialty publication will have the most ads for horses, but some will show up in the classified section of your newspaper. These are usually—but not always—the less valuable horses, owned by less experienced people. You may find good prospects in the local newspaper, but you're going to have to pick through a lot of overfed, undervaccinated, badly behaved backyard animals in order to uncover the good ones.

*Many horses for sale appear in classi-
fied ads; the best ones are listed in
specialized horse publications.*

An advertisement itself can provide helpful hints as to whether answering it is even worth your time. An ad that offers a "young phillie" may not be worth pursuing, and one that states that a horse "can be ridden" should make you wonder what he *can't* do.

Peruse the local paper's ads, but concentrate your efforts elsewhere. Ads in horse publications will offer you more suitable prospects and a lot more of them. There are often so many that you need to prescreen by learning to interpret the ads.

Some words send out warning flares regardless of what kind of horse you want. "Needs experienced rider," "spirited," and "exciting" can all describe difficult, even dangerous, horses. You should think carefully about buying such a horse even if you plan to use him in his original sport, but think it over very carefully if you hope to retrain such a horse as an adult. An uncontrollable horse may never concentrate well enough to learn anything new.

However, a horse can seem uncontrollable simply because he's uncomfortable with his tack or equipment or unable to execute the tasks he's being asked to perform. A change of career may bring a change of personality. If the ad describes an excitable horse that is promising in other ways, check him out.

Outgrown horses—always candidates for harness—will be described as "sadly outgrown" or "children's pet" or "small with a big heart." You have to watch out for spoiled nippers in this group, but you usually find good-natured animals that have been well treated.

A horse that is being sold along with all his tack is one that is not being replaced. This can be an "owner off to college" horse or a "no time to ride" situation, and the horse may be sound, well cared for, and worth your consideration.

A description of the horse's accomplishments in his sport or activity can also offer clues. An accomplished horse is probably one that is willing to learn more. If he "drives and rides" or "goes English and Western," he has already shown the mental and physical flexibility required for retraining. He may not even be very good at any of the activities, but at least he has shown himself to be trainable.

An ad that describes a horse's level of accomplishment in a given sport can often tell you if he has reached the final plateau in his sport and is ripe for retraining. A thirteen-year-old warmblood that is still at the training level in dressage may be conformed in such a way that he would be better off jumping, driving, or even performing a Western sport. A ten-year-old, 17-hand Thoroughbred advertised as a two-foot jumper is probably not much of a jumper at all and may be better on the flat.

What isn't said may also provide clues. A good-looking horse will almost always be advertised as "attractive," "handsome," or "cute." If looks aren't mentioned in an otherwise complete ad, the horse is probably plain. This won't matter if you want a usable animal, but it will if you hope to retrain him for a sport in which judges expect good looks.

"Good conformation" usually refers to conformation characteristics suited to the horse's breed or original sport. These may or may not be ideal for the sport you have in mind, so don't worry about looking for that description in the ads. If you find the word "correct" in an ad, make the phone call. A correct horse has good legs by the standards of any equine activity, so you can't go wrong (in leg soundness at least) with a horse described as such.

BULLETIN BOARDS

Ads placed on bulletin boards generally contain the same words and descriptions as those in newspapers. In fact, sellers often place the same ad in newspapers or horse magazines and on the bulletin board at the local feed store.

Some sellers do use bulletin boards exclusively. These owners are not usually as eager to sell, so they don't mind having a narrower audience for their ads. A horse in this category may be very low-priced, untrained, green, old, or have some other aspect which might lead a buyer to believe that he won't be very desirable. But sometimes the horse is desirable and the owner is willing to keep him indefinitely solely for sentimental reasons.

Retraining prospects can be found on bulletin boards in feed stores, tack shops, veterinary offices, or anywhere else that horse owners are likely to visit. A horse that didn't quite work out for someone, but is nice enough that the owner isn't desperate to unload him, could well work out for another person in a different use.

WORD OF MOUTH

Thousands of horses change hands each year because somebody told a friend that another friend had a horse for sale. Although a sale that doesn't work out can damage friendships, it's not a bad way to acquire a horse. Your friend may know something about the horse, will probably tell you the truth about why he is being sold, and can vouch for the owner.

You also might hear of horses for sale at lesson barns, boarding stables, horse shows, and other gathering places. You can also ask farriers and large animal vets about prospects (although they may be more likely to know about unsound horses). Tell all your horse-owning friends what you're looking for, and you will soon begin to get telephone calls from sellers.

RACETRACKS

Racetracks—Thoroughbred, Quarter Horse, and Standardbred—are filled with retraining prospects. Since hardly any of the stallions and only some of the mares will ever be used in breeding, the vast majority of racehorses will need to be retrained if they are going to survive past the age of eight or nine.

Some trainers, owners, and industry organizations do better than others in finding retraining homes for retiring racehorses. Each of the sports has humane groups organized with that purpose in mind, but these groups aren't active everywhere. Many sales (or giveaways) are

Racetracks provide thousands of retraining prospects each year.

informal, and you will have to contact trainers, trainers' groups, or race-track management to help you locate either a placement organization or an individual trainer with a horse to place.

Some horses that can no longer earn their keep on the track are placed in auctions. You will need to look for "Horses of Racing Age" sales, usually held at or near racetracks. Call for a catalog, which will describe the recent racing record of the horses. You will be looking for prospects that appear to be sound enough to race but slow enough that racing owners and trainers won't be interested.

For these sales, the horses are often not moved to the sale site until the day of the sale, so follow the auction house's instructions about pre-inspections. If you can talk to the trainer, do so. He or she will usually be honest with you about the horse's potential for retraining. Most of them got into the business because they love horses, so they are happy when one of their retirees goes to a good home rather than a slaughter-house.

Remember that you can often buy a catalogued horse privately before the auction (although somebody is going to have to pay a fee to the auction organizer). If the horse you like is a Standardbred pacer, don't worry abut facing a daunting retraining task. As you will see in Chapter Six, some of the best prospects of all fit into this category.

CHAPTER THREE

Evaluating the Retraining Prospect

I N SOME WAYS, EVALUATING A RETRAINING prospect is like evaluating any other potential purchase. But you will find that the steps you follow will be different.

When examining a horse that you intend to retrain for a new sport, you should look at his conformation the same way that you would in a horse bred for, or already trained in, your sport. You should also look at soundness, but the strictness of your guidelines for soundness may vary, depending on your goal. Test the horse for his previous training, but consider what he can learn rather than what he knows. Let's look at each category in greater detail.

CONFORMATION

If you ask experts in each of the equine sports to describe a well-conformed horse, you will probably hear nearly identical descriptions. But if you ask those same experts to point out an example of such a horse, they will show you remarkably different animals. This happens not because experts aren't as knowledgeable as they would like us to think, but because they (and we all) have to live with three basic facts of equine conformation.

First, there are certain qualities of structure that are universally desirable in every horse. Second, no horse possesses all of these desirable qualities; additionally, no horse is free from flaws.

The final fact is the most important with regard to retraining—differing requirements in various sports mean that you can enjoy great flexibility in your definition of an undesirable quality. If competitors in a particular sport see champion after champion with a certain physical characteristic in common, they are not going to consider that characteristic undesirable, even if it isn't quite in line with their idea of perfection.

You're not going to look at many near-perfect horses in your search for a retraining prospect. These horses are probably doing just fine in their original sports where they will invariably stay unless their personalities conflict with the activity.

But you do want to pay attention to the basic guidelines of good conformation. Standards have been established by generations of horse people studying many more generations of horses used in dozens of different activities. The closer a horse is to having ideal conformation, the more athletic he will be and the more likely he is to stay sound. If your

A balanced horse is the ideal, regardless of the sport.

sport demands great athleticism and soundness—eventing, hunting, roping, or similar activities—you are going to have to stay as close to the ideal as you possibly can.

What's "ideal"? The one word you hear more often than any other when you listen to discussions of good conformation is "balance." A balanced horse is one whose parts are in proportion to each other and to the whole.

You want a horse with a head that is neither too big nor too small and a neck of moderate length with a slight but not pronounced arch. You want a chest of reasonable width, a shoulder long enough to provide some slope, and a back short enough to be strong but long enough to be flexible. The hindquarters should be muscular, with the croup sloping enough to allow free movement behind. The length of the legs should be proportional to body size, set squarely underneath the horse, ending in symmetrical feet big enough to support the horse's weight.

This sounds simple enough. But the preceding describes both a good Clydesdale bred to pull a beer wagon *and* a fine Thoroughbred bred to win the Kentucky Derby. Obviously, "muscular" is going to mean different things to different people involved with those two horses, but experts in each category will be able to appreciate the balance and correctness of the near-perfect horse in the other.

Specialists in a specific sport are less willing and able to be objective about undesirable physical characteristics that may not be so undesirable in other sports. That's why some outstanding prospects are rejected by their own sports and become available for retraining. Take a look at individual body parts in terms of the horse's intended use as you examine your retraining prospects.

THE HEAD

Good horses are commonly rejected by owners because of unattractive heads, even though the head is the least important part of the horse in terms of soundness and usefulness. Occasionally, a horse with a poor head is discarded because the owner wants to compete in events where conformation counts. In such classes—and occasionally in classes where conformation isn't supposed to matter—an unattractive head will be penalized.

Very rarely, a badly sized head compromises athletic performance. A head so large that it's dramatically out of proportion to the rest of the body can limit a horse's potential in sports where the front end must act like a lever in helping transfer weight behind. A big-headed horse often has trouble in Western performance events that require a strong stop. The higher levels of dressage, which require extreme collection, are also difficult for a horse with a too-large head.

Conversely, a too-small head can sometimes be a disadvantage for a jumper as he tries to maintain good form over obstacles, since length and weight in front help the downward momentum. Driving horses may also do poorly if their heads are extremely small, since they need weight in front in order to pull effectively.

A calm, alert expression promises the
ability to learn.

Don't forget that a head poorly sized for one sport can be useful in another. The small-headed jumper may be good for dressage or Western use, while the horse with the big head may be able to jump and pull.

In spite of long-standing prejudices, Roman noses and pig eyes have no effect on performance. A horse that is well conformed except for a Roman nose is still well conformed, period. As for too-small eyes, there is no solid evidence that they have anything to do with intelligence or personality, in spite of an almost universal objection to them.

It is true that a calm, alert, and cheerful expression in a horse's eyes usually means that he is willing and trainable. Such a horse is probably a good candidate for retraining.

THE NECK

The shape and length of the neck are important to a horse's performance in most equine sports. A too-long or too-short neck has many of the same disadvantages as a mis-sized head and some additional problems for particular sports.

A properly proportioned neck is especially critical for horses ridden in Western pleasure and performance sports. A horse with a very short neck usually carries his head high to maintain balance, and this may prevent him from achieving the necessary shape for Western pleasure. But a long neck is not ideal either, since the extra body weight carried in front prevents the rear-end transfer of weight required for all Western horses, particularly in performance events like reining, cutting, and roping.

A slightly long-necked stock horse may be suitable for Western pleasure. A very long-necked one might be best tried out in jumping or driving.

Necks are important in dressage prospects, too. A very short neck almost guarantees that the horse will not have the kind of front-end flexibility required for anything beyond training level. But a neck that's too long will also limit a horse's progress. Flexibility is not a problem in long-necked horses, but head carriage is. The horse with a long neck will carry his head low, a shape suitable for low-level dressage. But the low head will prevent the collection needed at the higher levels.

Shape is just as important as length. A slight arch is attractive, and in some sports it's useful. In others, it's absolutely necessary. Don't expect dressage-style collection from a horse with a ewe-neck or one that carries more weight below than on top. If the weight is fat or untoned flesh, training will change the shape a little. If it's structure, he can't succeed. A concave neck is not very good for jumpers either, but even so, there have been some Olympic-level jumpers with no arch to speak of.

A flat or slight ewe-neck will probably be fine for Western sports and for most kinds of driving. An extreme concave line may require some experimentation with bits to maintain control, but the horse that possesses it should still be useful.

THE SHOULDER

Most horse people will say that they want a horse with a shoulder long enough to provide some slope, but the definition of "enough" varies dramatically from sport to sport. The slope of the shoulder controls the front-leg action, so opinions on length and slope are determined by the requirements of the sport.

In general, a short, straight shoulder leads to high action and short strides, while a long, sloping shoulder leads to long and low strides. Nonsprinting Thoroughbred racehorses almost always have very deep shoulders, while racing Quarter Horses (that need to take a lot of short strides very quickly) have straighter shoulders.

If you want to use a horse in a galloping sport like eventing or hunting, you need a horse with a sloping shoulder. A long shoulder is also important for sports that require extended gaits, like dressage.

If you need a horse that lifts his knees high, such as one to be used as a showy carriage or sleigh puller, look for a straighter shoulder. The straight shoulder also gives more pulling power, and so it is suitable for a driving horse with less dramatic action but a heavy burden to pull. The shoulder won't prevent the draft horse from being used for riding, but he probably will not be much of a galloper.

Draft breeds usually have straight shoulders—ideal for pulling, but not so good for galloping.

The short-shouldered horse is also good in most Western performance sports, since the short strides he produces increase maneuverability. Most good cutting, roping, and reining horses are fairly straight shouldered.

Short shoulders are often also wide, and saddle fitting for Quarter Horses and harness horses can sometimes be a challenge. Western saddles can be found with a Quarter Horse tree, and extra-wide English saddles can be found thanks to the increasing popularity of warmbloods with draft-type ancestors.

As for jumping, short shoulders can help a horse tuck up his knees in front, while long shoulders help him extend over wider spreads. The most useful jumper is probably the horse with average shoulders, but the other lengths can work too.

THE WITHERS

Wither height is usually related to shoulder length, with the long, sloping shoulders resulting in higher withers and short ones ending with low withers. There are exceptions among certain breeds. Many Percherons have comparatively short, straight shoulders but high and well-defined withers; whereas, most draft horses are built going downhill—with the croup higher than the withers.

Horses with long shoulders and prominent withers are desirable in dressage and other sports that require collection. For less demanding activities, the withers can be more important in terms of tack fitting. A horse with unusually high or low withers may need a breast collar or a crupper to keep the saddle in place.

THE BACK

The length of the back is important for soundness and performance. In some activities, back length is extremely important, while in others it's less of a consideration.

Shorter backs are less frequently subject to injury. A short-backed horse can usually carry more weight than a long-backed horse of similar size, and he can usually carry that weight over a longer distance. It's no surprise that Arabs, which have one less lumbar vertebra than other horses, dominate endurance riding competitions. So you should look for a short back in a horse you expect to ask to carry weight over a distance.

On the other hand, if your sport requires great flexibility, a short back can limit a horse's suppleness and his ability to bend. Stiffness caused by conformation can prevent a horse from reaching a high level in dressage. Some sports, such as Western performance events and polo, require both flexibility and weight-carrying ability. In this case, you want a horse with a fairly short back but good agility. The back shouldn't be too short, however. Western performance and polo often feature male riders, whose saddles might not fit a very short back.

A short-backed horse can still be flexible if his neck is not too thick.

Since body length helps prevent interference between front and hind legs, a long back is an advantage for a horse that is expected to produce a long-striding trot. A long back is less of an advantage but certainly no hindrance to harness horses that work at slower paces. Most harness breeds do have long backs as a result of generations of selection for noninterfering strides. There is one exception: Since fore-and-hind-leg interference isn't a factor in their gait, pacing Standardbreds are often short-backed. A pacer retrained for saddle use can often stay sound under a much heavier rider than other harness horses of similar size.

Among riding breeds, a horse with a back too long to stay sound under a rider can usually be driven successfully. Some long-backed horses, whether bred for harness or riding, can even stay sound under a great deal of weight. These animals' long backs are also broad and well-muscled. Many draft breeds qualify, and a long-legged, heavy rider should look at draft-type harness horses for a mount with a back long enough to fit him and sturdy enough to carry his weight.

THE HINDQUARTERS

The hindquarters form the power plant of the horse, so they are vital to every horse involved in any kind of athletic activity. The hindquarters are particularly important in sports requiring great impulsion, such as jumping and galloping, and in those requiring sudden starts and stops, such as Western performance events. Strong hindquarters are also important to harness horses, because they use their rear ends to provide the weight to stop themselves and their vehicles. Following is what you need to consider when you look at the hindquarters of a retraining prospect.

The croup—the topline of the hindquarters when viewed from the side—is usually considered to be in ideal balance when its high point is the same height as the withers. Any variation from balance will affect a horse's ability to perform a sport, but sometimes a croup higher or lower than the withers may actually help.

A horse higher at the croup than the withers will find classic collection difficult. It's hard for such a horse to transfer his center of balance away from the forehand. But a higher croup is a slight advantage in most of the Western performance sports and in polo, since these sports require a horse to be extremely agile as he starts, stops, and turns from his haunches. A lower front end is more maneuverable and allows weight—as opposed to simple balance—to be transferred behind.

The opposite is also true, of course. Withers higher than the croup are acceptable and even desirable for dressage but are a serious detriment to the "start-and-stop" sports.

Look next at the shape of the croup. In general, you want a modest slope from the high point of the croup to the root of the tail for best performance; although Arabs and Saddlebreds do just fine with very flat croups.

In some sports, croups with slopes well beyond modest are found on good horses. A sloping croup helps rear-end collection, so many high-level dressage horses have them. A horse intended to run a distance can prosper with a sloping croup because it helps produce a long, sweeping stride at the gallop.

Jumpers vary. Some good jumpers have dramatically sloping croups, a few have flat ones, and many have modest slopes. Some experts, particularly old-time ones, believe that a horse with a dramatic slope to his croup, topped by a bump at the high point, will have jumping talent. This "jumper's bump" does appear on some good horses, but it also appears on others that can't jump their own shadows.

Next, look at the hindquarters from behind. In most sports, the width of the hindquarters is important only when they are so wide or so narrow that they affect placement of the legs. Hind legs placed too close can interfere, and legs placed too far apart can create an awkward and inefficient gait.

High withers and a slight slope to the croup are ideal for dressage.

Horses intended for the start-and-stop sports do need fairly broad hindquarters for the sudden impulsion required in most of the events, but if they're too wide, they can compromise agility. Most harness breeds have wide hindquarters, too. A horse intended for endurance events will do better with hindquarters that tend towards the narrow, because they will have less body weight to carry over the distance.

THE LEGS

Sound and well-constructed legs are more important than any other part of the horse, and the more demanding the intended sport, the more important his legs are to his success. A horse intended for light pleasure riding—walking and trotting only over moderate distances—can often have poorly conformed legs. This is not so for a horse that is intended to run, jump, change direction, and go a distance, so if you are planning these activities for your retrained horse, look at the joints first.

The perfect knee, viewed from the side, should be in the middle of a straight line running from the center of the forearm to the front of the cannon bone. This conformation produces a strong leg, a long stride, and the ability to fold up the knees, characteristics needed in running, jumping, and high action under harness.

There are two general variations from the ideal, one of which is of minor importance, while the other is a serious flaw. First, there's the horse that is described as "over at the knee." His lower leg stands noticeably behind his forearm and knee, creating a backward angle or convex shape. Although being over at the knee will limit a horse's potential in conformation classes, it usually does not affect his ability to run or jump. Unless very extreme, it usually has no effect on long-term soundness, either. Many very successful Thoroughbred racehorses are over at the knee, and some trainers even believe that these animals stay sounder than ones with more correct forelegs.

The other flaw is much more serious. The horse that possesses this is described as "back at the knee" or "calf-kneed." This foreleg forms a concave shape when viewed from the side, with the knee set back from an imaginary line that connects the top of the leg with the hoof. The knee may be so far back that it appears to be almost under the belly. This conformation places tremendous stress on the ankle joint, the pastern, and the tendons and ligaments at the back of the cannon bone. Don't expect to do much running or jumping with this horse, but he would probably stay sound under harness.

Viewed from the front, the ideal legs should drop straight down to the hooves from either side of the center of the chest. Knee flaws seen here include nonsquare knees which produce lower legs that turn either in or out. This leads to feet that turn in or out at the toe, and either condition can make it difficult for the front legs to stay sound under stress. Jumping is most stressful to the forelegs, followed by galloping. If you plan to do either, look for a horse as correct as possible when looking at his forelegs from the front.

Occasionally, you will find a horse that toes in or out on one side only. These horses sometimes have odd movement at the canter and gallop, with one foreleg winging out, paddling, or dishing. This usually makes a horse unsuitable for dressage, and it can be a problem in a sport that requires tight turns. But unless it's extreme, pleasure horses manage well. Many good jumpers also have nonsquare knees on one side, and most learn to land properly.

The knee joint itself should be well defined and reasonably large. Except in the case of swollen joints, size means strength. Good, big knees are valuable in sports that stress the front end rather than the rear, so big knees are important on a would-be jumper, while smaller ones are acceptable on a Western performance horse.

The hock, the rear-end equivalent of the knee, suffers from similar flaws, plus a few of its own. Conduct the examination of the hock the same way you did the knee. From the side, check the placement of the hock in relation to the hindquarters. The ideally balanced hock will permit you to draw an imaginary straight line from the back of the buttock through the point of the hock, continuing down the back of the hind leg.

Hocks placed further under or further back are common, and some have their uses. A hock placed forward of that line produces a straight hind leg, which some horsemen believe helps a horse to jump. It's also not entirely undesirable in a galloping horse. A hock that's a little more crooked is an advantage in the start-and-stop sports, since it contributes to sideways agility. But excessive bend can lead to unsoundness.

Viewed from behind, the midpoint of each buttock, the middle of the hock, and the middle of the fetlock should be in a straight line. If the hocks turn out, the horse is bowlegged behind. He will lack flexibility and be subject to hock injury. Hocks that turn in produce the cow-hocked horse. This is rarely a problem in horses intended for Western performance or harness events, unless the harness use requires high action at the trot. Nonsquare hocks tend to produce low action behind.

Let's move on to the pastern, the concussion-absorbing part of the leg. Ideal slope and length are different for the front and rear legs. On the nonexistent "perfect horse," a front pastern should be moderately long, with a 45-degree slope from the fetlock joint, through the pastern, and continuing on through the hoof. The back pastern should be slightly straighter.

In the real world, pasterns are often longer or shorter than moderate, with a slope less or greater than 45 degrees. A short, straight pastern transfers the shock and concussion that occurs whenever a hoof strikes the ground further up the leg, leading to knee unsoundness. Jumpers and runners need longer pasterns with more slope, but these slopy pasterns can cause great stress to the tendons behind the cannon bone. Endurance horses often do well with fairly short, upright pasterns, and Western performance horses often stay sounder if their pasterns tend towards short rather than long, although it's the slope rather than the length that is significant.

All athletic horses should have fairly big, uniform feet, but horses whose work can cause concussion need them in particular. The front feet of horses that are intended to jump are especially important. A would-be jumper with feet that are too small for his body size might look graceful, but he will probably not remain sound in front. In the start-and-stop sports, rear feet are just as important as front. Small feet are visually appealing on a Western horse, but larger ones are far sounder.

Uniformity is important too, particularly for the physically demanding events. You probably won't find a horse with four matching feet, so your goal should be to find a horse with two matching pairs of feet—the front feet should be similar as should the hind feet. Horses with unmatching or too-small feet are best used in sports that don't place much concussion on the hooves, such as pleasure competitions, trail riding, or driving.

THE HEALTH CHECK

Try to obtain a prepurchase veterinarian check for any disease or medical condition that will limit the horse's use. Even if the horse doesn't cost much, his transportation and care will, and it's obviously preferable to pay a little in advance than to pay a lot later.

You can ask for a health examination that's either expensive and very complete or cheap and simple. The first will probably tell you if the horse you're considering is infected with contagious disease or has a problem that's incurable and progressive. The second will help you identify less serious problems that will affect the horse's potential. Whichever exam you choose, be sure to inform the veterinarian of how you intend to use the horse. An insurmountable problem in one sport may be no concern at all in another.

Once active disease is ruled out, soundness becomes your main consideration. You can do some of the soundness check yourself. The first and simplest thing to do is to watch the horse stand quietly. How he carries his weight on his four legs will tell you something about his physical comfort. Although some horses almost always rest a hind leg while standing, no sound horse will rest a foreleg. A horse that shifts his weight a little too often may be uncomfortable.

Have someone walk the horse and watch for hitches in the gait, an irregularly nodding head, or other signs of lameness. Sometimes you can hear what you can't see, so walking the horse on a hard surface may make lameness obvious.

Trotting will bring out even more potential lameness, particularly if you can watch the horse trot in a circle, once in each direction. The inside leg takes stress in this situation, and soreness may show up.

Evenly worn hooves suggest a sound horse whose feet are suitable for work.

Look at the feet for signs of uneven wear on the shoes or on the horn of the hoof itself. Take advantage of any chance to watch a farrier shoe or trim the horse. If he doesn't have to do corrective shoeing or even out irregular growth or wear, you are probably looking at a sound horse. Picking up the feet and gently flexing the fetlocks, the knees, and the hocks may also reveal stiffness, swelling, or pain that hasn't shown up otherwise.

A veterinarian can take radiographs of joints, bones, and feet. This should certainly be done with an expensive horse that you plan to use in a demanding sport. If you or your veterinarian determine that the horse is sound enough for your plans, move on to other observations.

GROUND OBSERVATION

You can learn a great deal about a horse's potential for a sport and a little about his previous training without riding or driving him. But bear a couple of points in mind as you observe the horse. First, remember that a horse's physical movements cannot be exactly the same when he has weight on or behind him as they are when he's at liberty in a field. And second, a horse may behave entirely differently when handled by an unmounted person than while being ridden or driven. Still, ground observation can give you important clues.

THE HORSE AT LIBERTY

If your prospect can be turned out (preferably with other horses), watch him closely for as much time as you can spare. The best time to watch is just as he's released, when he is most likely to be active and energetic. At liberty, the horse will show you the physical movement most natural to him, and he will demonstrate the balance, flexibility, mobility, and speed that he is able to produce. He will also show his enthusiasm for movement—a quality vital to the athletic horse.

Observing a horse at liberty can give you a good idea of his balance, gaits, and athleticism.

Some horses also show natural collection and extension, so if you hope to do dressage with the horse you're watching, look for the movements that promise the talents you need. If you're looking for a horse to use in a sport that requires agility, you may see that in the field as well. You may also see a clumsy horse with stiff gaits. This doesn't mean that the horse can't be trained for the sport, but it may indicate that you will have a lot more work ahead of you.

It's rare that you will see a horse jump while he's turned out in a field; adult horses rarely jump for the fun of it. There is information to be obtained from liberty jumping though, so some trainers will set up a chute to force an untrained jumper to clear an obstacle. This activity usually resembles a comedy of errors, with a frightened or annoyed horse trying to go anywhere but over the jump. A liberty jump can show you a horse's natural flexibility in the knees, allowing him to fold his forelegs, and it can show you whether he's inclined to drag his hind legs. It can give you an indication of scope and tell you whether he's likely to be able to learn to jump wide as well as high.

Whether you watch a horse turned out in a field or forced over a liberty jump, there is one big problem: At liberty, he has no weight on his back. His balance is different, the demands on his muscles and limbs are different, and his attitude is different. In the field, he's doing what he chooses, while under a rider, he's doing what the rider chooses. The horse at liberty will give you a hint, but he's making no promises.

GROUND HANDLING

How the horse handles on the ground will also give you a hint about his previous training and his trainability. Again, there are no promises. Some horses are angelic without a rider or driver and devilish with one.

But a horse with good basic training and a pleasant, pro-human attitude will show it as you handle him for normal stable activities and transportation. Catching may be excepted (the most saintly of horses sometimes play games before being caught in the field), but a trainable horse will allow himself to be haltered, led, touched, and tacked up.

The more handling his new sport will require, the more important it is for you to make sure he doesn't fight being touched, prodded, and used. Driving requires patience and docility on the part of the horse, since harnessing and hooking up can be complicated. A nervous horse that always jumps when he's touched may not be a good harness prospect.

Many of the Western performance sports require a horse that's both attentive and calm, since most require patient waiting before a sudden burst out of a starting box. Ground handling can clue you in to whether or not your horse has these qualities. Watch the horse's reaction to sights and sounds as you lead him around, stop him, and touch him. If he's cooperative but fully aware of what's going on, he may be what you want.

On the other hand, Western pleasure and most trail use require horses that pay almost no attention to any extraneous noises or sights and seem oblivious to everyone except their riders. This kind of horse can often be identified while leading and tacking.

A horse destined for a new sport that will require training for difficult skills, such as advanced dressage, should give you the impression that he's intelligent enough to learn. See if he knows how to stand properly for an examination. He may already know, but if he doesn't, he should be able to learn the basics in a few seconds. Move him into a specific position and ask that he stay. If he can figure out this easy demand quickly, he probably has the intelligence and willingness to learn.

If you intend to use the horse in a sport that requires trailering, see how much he's learned about loading and traveling. You can teach a poor traveler to behave on the road, but it can be a long and difficult process with an adult horse. You may want the horse anyway, but you should know in advance that your retraining job will be even bigger than expected.

As with liberty observation, ground handling will give you an idea but no guarantees about your retraining prospect. A ride or drive, even on a horse that knows nothing about your intended sport, will give you an even better idea.

THE TEST

Even though your plans for a horse may be far different from the work he currently does, experiencing him under saddle or harness will help you in making your decision. It will also furnish you with an important first step in your retraining project.

THE PROCEDURE TO FOLLOW

ASK QUESTIONS

The horse's previous owner or trainer can tell you a lot about his skills, talents, and habits. Don't be too shy to ask, even if the horse is coming off the racetrack or is listed in an upcoming auction. The worst you'll be told is that nobody knows anything about him. Most owners will have at least a little something to say. Just remember that you may not get an entirely realistic description if you haven't yet bought the horse.

First ask what the horse could do when he was acquired. You may discover that he used to do exactly what you intend for him, and you'll be looking at tuning up old skills rather than retraining for new ones.

Ask next what the horse learned to do for his owner. The new skills—both their number and complexity—will tell you about his learning potential as well as his current skill level. The owner may also tell you about habits or quirks that you would otherwise have to discover for yourself. He or she may have already worked out solutions to tack-fitting problems, allergies, pet peeves, or something else that might affect your training plans.

ASK THE OWNER TO RIDE OR DRIVE

If circumstances permit, ask the previous owner to ride or drive the horse while you watch. You will probably see the horse at his best, particularly if the sale isn't yet final. Even though the sport may be different, you will be able to observe willingness, attitude, and athleticism—important characteristics if your intended sport is demanding.

Two kinds of previous owners may give you an inaccurate picture of the horse's accomplishments. One is the highly skilled rider who makes the horse's responses appear effortless. The other is the terrible rider who makes the horse fight and resist.

You will be able to identify either kind of rider quickly. But a ride by either isn't a waste of everybody's time. You will be able to observe the horse's general movement and natural balance. Just remember that he may be neither as easy nor as difficult to train and handle as he appears. In either case, you will then move on to the next step in assessing your prospect.

RIDE OR DRIVE YOURSELF

You will find it very useful to ride or drive the horse, even if he's not trained for your sport and you're not trained for his. If you are unable to ride or drive and that is all the horse can do, ask a friend whose horse judgment you trust to perform the test for you.

This initial assessment doesn't have to be elaborate. Later, after you have decided on the horse and your retraining program, you will look a little more closely at the horse's current level of knowledge and skill. In fact, an extensive assessment will be a vital first step in the retraining process. But at this point, you're looking at general attitude and response.

Any broken adult horse will know how to start, steer, and stop. These are skills you are going to test. One warning: If your horse has been trained Western and is outfitted with a high-ported curb or an even more severe bit for your test, don't use an English-style direct rein when turning him and don't ride with the same kind of contact you would use with a snaffle. This would not be fair to the horse, and he might fight, pull, and behave poorly in general because of unfamiliar rough treatment. Many Western horses do know how to direct rein and will accept contact, but they won't respond well with a severe bit.

As you ride or drive, study the horse's responses to your requests. Since you are not asking for anything difficult, you won't be judging the skill with which the horse executes your requests, but rather the attitude and speed of his responses.

A good retraining prospect won't lag, toss his head, and be annoyed with the entire process. He will respond quickly to the signals you give him even if he doesn't do exactly what you would expect from a horse trained in your sport.

If you have the time and the inclination you can test the horse at all gaits, in figure eights, with lead changes, and for other more advanced skills. These more complex requests will help tell you if the horse might have the talent for his intended sport and not just a willingness to learn. He may show you the agility needed for Western performance, the balance needed for dressage, or the strong forward momentum required for driving.

PART TWO

Western and English

CHAPTER FOUR

Western to English

THE CHANGE FROM WESTERN TO ENGLISH riding will force you to change your horse's tack and force him to transform his physical style and alter his attitude. Just how much he's going to have to change depends on the level of English riding you plan for the horse. This chapter will cover the change from the most basic level of Western to the most basic of English—the move from Western pleasure or Western riding to English hack or hunter on the flat. If you plan to move your Western-trained horse on to jumping or dressage, that comes after he masters the basics of English style riding.

WHY CHANGE?

Most owners who move their horses from Western to English do so for the simplest reason—they ride English and they have acquired a horse trained for Western use. Sometimes the reason is a little more complicated. Perhaps they own or have acquired a Western horse not ideally suited for Western riding. These horses tend to fit into one of two categories. Some have conformation characteristics that limit their performance, while others have personality traits that do the same.

Sometimes a horse will have both. Moja Matka, an eleven-year-old Arab mare, was trained from her first days under saddle as a Western pleasure horse. She learned well, becoming a consistent ribbon winner. But she liked to move out, had what appeared to be a natural hard mouth, and required a big curb bit with a high port to keep her at the slow pace necessary for Western pleasure. More important, she developed a back injury because she did not have the flat topline required for Western pleasure.

After eight years of showing Western, rider and trainer Judy Nixon decided to make the switch to English. The move might have come at the beginning of Moja's career had Arab shows been featuring more hunters.

"At the time, Western pleasure was the way to go, because English hunters were undesirable," Nixon says. "Now, it's the other way around."

The move paid off. Moja and Nixon were winners in their first show under English tack. If Moja had been a trail or companion horse, there would have been no need to retrain. Her personality and shape might have encouraged the English choice right from the beginning of her working life.

WHICH HORSES SHOULD CHANGE?

Any horse can make the basic change to English, no matter how much he looks like a stock horse. If you have no ambitions to show against horses actually bred for English riding, it won't matter how low his withers, how wide his hindquarters, or how muscular his chest might be. If you do want to show, there are more and more hunter classes in shows for stock breeds.

Some Western-bred horses are more likely than others to be suited to English use. Because an appendix has been added to the Quarter Horse stud book allowing horses with one Thoroughbred parent, there are now many registered Quarter Horses with more Thoroughbred than Quarter Horse blood. As a result you may find among any modern group of Quarter Horses plenty of animals more suited to English hunter style than to traditional Western uses.

Both the Appaloosa and Paint Horse associations also register horses with Thoroughbred parents. Thoroughbred breeding was once actively encouraged in an effort to produce refined racing animals. Although Appaloosa and Paint racing haven't proven to be as popular as hoped, Thoroughbred blood has been successful in contributing long

Horses of all breeds, even Quarter Horses and Paints, perform well as English hunter mounts.

necks, sloping shoulders and croups, and occasional straight hocks to these stock breeds too.

Several breeds have been used and shown both English and Western for decades. People who ride Arabs and Morgans have outlets in breed shows for both styles. Each breed also has a third outlet—the high-action park or English pleasure style—and horses that lack the action are made Western horses. Some of these, like Moja Matka, are superb candidates for retraining.

TACK

Before you mount the horse for testing or retraining, consider the tack you plan to use. You may decide to make a complete and abrupt switch from the horse's familiar tack, or you may prefer a complete but gradual switch. You may even conclude that a partial switch is the best way to go.

THE SADDLE

One item will require a complete change, but with careful fitting and preparation the horse will hardly notice the difference. This is the saddle, the most noticeable difference between the riding styles, but one that is easily changed for most horses.

Two aspects of saddle choice are of concern to retrainers. The first is the fact that an English saddle, with the exception of the specialized dressage and saddle-seat saddles, places the rider's weight much further forward and considerably closer to the horse than the Western saddle.

Stock-type horses usually have wide shoulders and broad chests and should be able to handle a lighter saddle, which will put more weight nearer to the shoulders. But if such a horse has been used under a saddle that sits higher and nearer to the center of the back, he has probably developed strong muscles over the back in order to suit that weight distribution. The horse may have great strength in the loins but less strength in the muscles immediately behind the shoulders and withers.

The solution is simple. The horse should be allowed to adjust to a change in weight distribution gradually—even over a period of weeks and months—no matter how quickly the other adjustments to the new style are made. A light rider can probably manage a less gradual transition, but a heavy rider should be particularly careful of an abrupt change.

Some trainers find it worthwhile to alternate saddles—English one day, Western the next—as the horse is trained to his new rein and neck aids. This allows the back and shoulder muscles to develop slowly without delaying the retraining process. If you don't own or can't borrow a Western saddle, or if you are convinced that the horse is sturdy enough to adjust immediately, keep the training sessions short at first and lengthen them as the horse develops new muscles.

Fitting an English saddle will be equally important. Certainly, proper fitting is vital with any horse and any saddle, but you may find particular problems with the Western to English change. The low withers and short, wide shoulders of many stock-type horses can make an adventure out of saddle fitting. Many English saddles with a regular tree—especially extreme forward-seat jumping saddles—are designed for horses with much narrower and higher withers. These saddles will perch too high on the backs of many stock horses and will be uncomfortable for both horse and rider.

Jumping saddles are available with wide trees, but these are usually designed for warmblood horses that are taller and bigger overall. They may or may not fit a short, stock-type horse. The other nondressage English saddle, usually described as all-purpose or event, is also available with a wide tree. This saddle has straighter panels and usually fits wider shoulders somewhat better than the close contact, but much depends on the design of the particular tree and the flexibility of the panels.

In either case, try to find a saddle that fits. A good quality saddle with a too-narrow tree can sometimes be made wider by a skilled saddle repairman, but it may be more practical to shop around for a new one. A stretched-out wire coat hanger shaped over the withers at the point where the front of the saddle will rest can be taken to the tack shop and fitted to the available saddles. A shop with return privileges is important if you're shopping for an English saddle for stock horses. Some manufacturers have developed treeless and flexible-tree saddles designed to fit a wider range of horses with bigger or smaller than normal shoulders and withers. The jury is still out on the long-term performance of nontraditional saddles, but they may prove useful for the difficult-to-fit horse.

A horse with very low withers but not particularly wide shoulders may need extra equipment to keep an English saddle from slipping forward if your plans include any downhill riding. Riding cruppers, which fasten the saddle to a strap that goes around the tail, can occasionally be found at tack shops. Otherwise, you can adapt a driving crupper.

Most saddles will require a saddle pad. Judy Nixon uses two while training Moja Matka, finding them particularly important to protect her withers during her switch to an English saddle.

Any low-withered horse will need similar attention. For such a horse, several pads may become part of his permanent equipment while

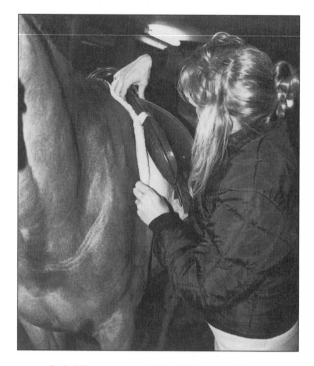

*Judy Nixon uses careful padding to make sure
the English saddle fits the withers.*

being ridden English. But even a horse with higher withers will need one thick or two thinner pads during the early months of wearing an unfamiliar saddle. He will need to toughen up in different places because the pressure points differ in English and Western equipment.

You can offer the horse some familiarity on the girth. Western and English girths have different names, fasten differently, and are not interchangeable, but they can be made of similar materials. Although your Western-trained horse almost certainly did not use a leather or vinyl front cinch, he may have been ridden with a string cinch, a synthetic fleece cinch, or even a cotton webbing one. Ask the previous owner if one material proved better than others with the horse.

Some Western horses are ridden with a second cinch, a leather strap that fastens several inches further towards the hindquarters than the front cinch. There is no equivalent in English riding, and your Western-trained horse will not regret its absence.

THE BRIDLE

The difference between English and Western bridles has narrowed dramatically in recent decades. In fact, many Western horses are trained on English bridles and bits, and some continue using them throughout their lives.

Years ago the Western-trained horse, familiar only with a single-strap headstall with nothing more than a slit for one ear, might have been surprised and annoyed if you were to put a throatlatch, browband, and noseband on his head. Nowadays, he almost certainly will have been trained and ridden with a throatlatch, probably a browband, and often a noseband.

The noseband will have been plain unless he was used for roping or speed sports. He probably never experienced anything like a figure-eight or dropped noseband, and he may find these distracting if you choose to use them in his new career.

The browband and throatlatch will have been the same, as will the cheek pieces of the bridle, although his Western rider probably fastened them more loosely, allowing the bit to be carried lower in his mouth. He will not have been bridled with wrinkles in the corners of his mouth. The Western-trained horse would certainly prefer that you do this with his English bridle, too. But a snaffle that fits as loosely as a Western curb would probably permit him to get his tongue over the bit, so you are going to have to fasten it a little tighter than he might like. Until he's used to it, you will have to be particularly careful not to cause him pain. Even though he may be an experienced old horse with a hard mouth, he may not be hard in the corners.

The bit itself represents the most significant change of equipment you and your horse will face, although it probably won't be as dramatic a change as it would have been a few decades ago. The most basic and common English bit is the jointed snaffle. The basic Western bit is the unjointed curb, usually with a port rising over the tongue, but sometimes flat.

In the past, a Western horse may have been put directly into a curb or the even more severe spade as soon as he was broken. A more gently broken horse might have used a bitless hackamore, or bosal bridle, first and then advanced to the curb. At no point would the horse have learned to respond to pressure on one side of the mouth as a signal to turn.

Today the carefully broken Western horse will most likely have begun his training in a common English-style snaffle, and he will have learned the basics of turning, stopping, and backing in response to a mild, jointed bit. If your Western-trained horse is young, he may not yet have progressed to a curb bit and you can just continue using the snaffle, moving on later to a more challenging English bit if you find it necessary.

Even if your horse used a curb, it may actually have been a Western snaffle, a bit with curb-style cheeks and a snaffle mouth. In this case,

Judy Nixon chose a kimber-wicke for Moja Matka's English career to provide the control she experienced in her Western curb.

the change to a ringed snaffle will be simple. The pressure on the sides of the mouth will be the same, even though the lower cheekpieces of the jointed curb do create a leverage and a more severe action in the bit.

If the horse required a strong bit while ridden Western, you may find—as Judy Nixon did with Moja Matka—that an English bit similar in feel and effect to a Western curb is the answer.

"She was naturally stiff and hard-mouthed, from the first time I got on her. She really needed a big port," Nixon says, "so it was easy for me to pick one. I put her right into a kimberwicke." The ported kimberwicke, a kind of pelham that acts as a combination of snaffle and curb, provides a similar level of control as the Western curb as well as a familiar feel in the horse's mouth. The D-ring of the kimberwicke also gives a neat hunter look to the horse's head while giving greater control than a simple D-ring snaffle.

Regardless of the final bit you plan to use on your retrained horse, you will probably begin with a snaffle since it encourages the higher head carriage desirable in English style. It is also the easiest bit on both horse and rider, and you may find, as Nixon does, that your horse trains best on the snaffle.

"I school on a snaffle, I warm the horse on a snaffle, and only then go on to the show bit," Nixon says.

BRIDLE ADD-ONS

Western horses are sometimes trained and used with martingales, and if you plan to use one with your horse you may discover that he adjusts quickly and comfortably. As a Western horse, he might have used a tie-down, the Western equivalent of a standing martingale. The tie-down connects a separate noseband on the bridle to the cinch or girth. The general effects of the tie-down and the standing martingale are the same, preventing head tossing and a too-high head carriage, but the Western version attaches to a more severe cable noseband.

The running martingale, the more flexible English device, has no direct equivalent in Western riding. With its two straps that attach to moveable rings on the reins, it allows headset control through pressure on the mouth rather than the top of the nose.

Because of its usefulness and because there is no widely used Western version, many Western trainers have turned to standard running martingales right out of the English tack stores in training their horses. They are particularly popular in the early snaffle period of the training of a Western horse, and your horse may be familiar with them.

You should not use a martingale with your Western-trained horse unless you have evidence that you need one. Most Western horses making the switch to English need to have their heads raised rather than lowered, and the primary function of most martingales is to lower the head. A head tosser, bit evader, or rearer may need one, or he might work better in a specialty noseband. Check the horse under saddle before you make the decision.

THE FIRST RIDE

With your equipment chosen, you are ready to see what your horse knows how to do. Unless you have ridden him before taking him home or have been assured by someone you trust that the horse is easily rideable, have someone nearby ready to help in case the horse proves to be less trained than you thought.

MOUNTING

The differences between English and Western riding appear before you even get on the horse. The most common methods of mounting are different in each style, although the Western method is an acceptable alternative in English riding and vice versa.

Your Western horse will probably have been mounted in his previous career by a rider standing on his left side facing the saddle, putting the left foot in the stirrup and grasping the horn to pull himself aboard. The preferred English style has the rider, still on the left side, facing the rear of the horse and, grasping the far side flap on the saddle, swinging the right leg up and over the saddle.

The direction the rider is facing while on the ground makes no difference to the horse, but the Western style does allow horse and rider to be ready to move out immediately. The Western-trained horse may have even been trained to do so as soon as the rider is off the ground. This is unacceptable in English riding and undesirable in most Western riding. If you don't want it done, remember to take up the reins firmly as you mount. Don't pull back too sharply, however, or the horse might start backing sooner than you would expect an English-trained horse to do. Even though you now have the horse in a snaffle, he may remember the effects of a pull back in a curb.

MOVING FORWARD

Your initial ride is designed to determine what your horse has learned to do under his previous owners and trainers. This first test should ask simple things of the horse. At this point, you're trying to discover his foundation of training and his overall attitude. If he does know how to do more advanced movements, you will have time to discover and develop them as you continue your program.

Check first to see if your horse can be collected. A horse trained for Western pleasure showing and most Western performance sports probably understands the concept. Pull back very slightly on the reins and squeeze gently with both legs on or just behind the girth. If the horse backs, you have either pulled too hard or given a signal that he doesn't understand. If he does understand, he will flex his neck slightly and prepare his muscles.

Continue the squeeze, loosen the reins, and move out. If he has never been taught preparatory collection, loosen your reins, press a little harder on the girth, give him a verbal cue, and then move out.

STEERING

Almost all Western horses are trained to neck rein as their primary mode of steering. Many Western horses also respond to a direct rein, since early training on a snaffle is so common. Assuming that you are now riding in a snaffle, pull gently on the rein on the side you want to turn. If the horse responds quickly and properly, you have a horse that understands direct reining.

If he doesn't respond, you may have to make a more exaggerated motion, although you shouldn't have to pull any harder. Western direct reining, called plowlining by Western traditionalists, calls for the rein to be held fairly wide from the horse. Continue trying the direct rein until you find the point at which he responds.

If the horse simply doesn't respond to the direct rein, he may be an animal that was put directly into a curb or possibly into a bitless hackamore and then into the curb, and knows only to respond to the feel of the rein on the opposite side of the neck from the requested direction of his turn. If this is the case, you will have to follow the retraining procedures outlined later in this chapter.

TESTING THE LEG AIDS

At the basic training level, Western and English leg aids are usually identical. This is invariably true in the breeds that are commonly trained both English and Western, such as Arabs and Morgans. The primary leg signal to turn in both is slight pressure on the side of the girth in the direction you are going plus slight pressure behind the girth on the opposite side to keep the hindquarters turning in the same arc as the front of the body.

Some Western horses are trained without a leg aid on the turning side. Others, particularly those in the performance sports, are sometimes taught to turn only with leg aids. Although these horses almost always know how to respond to the neck rein also, they may not have done it recently, so they may be slow. Try the leg aids individually and together with neck reining, with direct reining, and with no reining in order to see what your horse can do.

LEADS

English and Western horses are usually also taught to take the correct lead in the canter, or lope, with the same aids. In each style, the rider asks for a left leading leg by turning the head slightly to the right and pressing behind the girth on the right side while urging the horse into the gait. This is probably how your horse will know how to choose his lead if he isn't allowed to make the decision himself.

As an English horse, Moja Matka is asked for the lead at the canter in the same way she was as a Western pleasure horse.

Some trainers in each style don't like the idea of turning the head and prefer to urge a correct lead with the leg only. At the more advanced levels of training in both Western and English use, the leg pressure becomes nearly imperceptible and head direction remains straight. A horse very well trained in his previous career may find the head-turning lead signal clumsy and annoying. In addition, advanced horses in each style are taught to change leads while cantering and galloping. The signals for these flying changes are slightly different in each discipline.

At the basic level, though, the aids are the same. Some Western horses are so good at picking the correct lead for turns by themselves that you won't be able to tell whether or not they're actually accepting your signals. Agile little Quarter Horses are known for this. If you want to know about your horse's responsiveness to the aids for the lead, you will have to test him on a straightaway.

PACE

Slow back to the walk to check the horse's preferred pace. Western horses, particularly those shown in Western pleasure classes, are trained to go quite slowly at all gaits. Some people want to speed up the pace in many of these classes, but the pace will still be much slower than the English rider is accustomed to. Try various degrees of leg pressure to judge the flexibility of the horse in his choice of pace. At the same time, check his reaction to the higher level of contact with his mouth. Although the snaffle bit is milder than his familiar curb, he may object to the feeling of greater contact.

HEAD CARRIAGE

Western riding generally calls for a lower head carriage and a more horizontal overall outline than that which is desirable in an English horse. You will be able to judge general head-carriage tendencies from the

A higher head carriage and topline were more comfortable for Moja Matka than the Western pleasure shape had been.

horse's back, but you may want to ask a friend to ride while you watch from the ground.

In some cases, such as that of Moja Matka, the Western pleasure head carriage wasn't natural to the horse's personality and conformation. Her head came right up when she was permitted to raise it.

STOPPING AND BACKING

Both Western and English training teach horses to halt with a firm but forgiving pull-back on the reins and a slight amount of leg pressure to prepare for the stop. Because Western horses often have to stop suddenly and thoroughly in their sports, they are sometimes also taught to halt immediately with a noticeable squeeze just in front of the girth and a lifting of the reins. This signals the horse to get his hindquarters well underneath him, a necessary movement in a sliding stop.

Some horses are either trained to or develop the habit of stopping to a lifting of the reins only. You will not find this desirable for hunter-style riding, particularly if you need to raise your hands to lift the head. At this point, you should check to see if your horse stops with a lift of the reins. Check also to see if he will stop with just the pull of the reins or if he requires pressure of the legs to ask for his halt.

Backing in both styles is accomplished with a forgiving rein and a gentle squeeze on or just behind the girth. Your horse should respond to your familiar aids.

After the preliminary ride decide which areas need no work, which need some, and which need a lot. In order to develop a complete and balanced English horse, pay attention to each aspect in every training session even though you will spend more time on the trouble areas than on the problem-free ones.

THE RETRAINING PROGRAM

Three facts about the nature of horses should remain in your mind throughout retraining. First, horses learn by repetition. Second, horses are comfortable with routine. And third, horses enjoy stimulation, just like other living creatures. The older the horse, the less he will find stimulating about basic training. So your goal should be to ask him to repeat his new skills often enough for them to become part of his routine under saddle, but ask him with enough variety in the daily program to keep him involved and interested. Start first with the area most likely to need work.

REINING

If your horse was well trained on the snaffle before learning neck reining, you won't have to do major work here. Just use careful and clear, direct rein signals as you work on other aspects of the horse's performance. If he neck reins exclusively or if he neck reins better than he direct reins, you will have to work out a program for him. The process will be far quicker and simpler than it would be for a young, green horse.

Your preliminary ride should have told you about the horse's responses to your requests to turn. Your retraining procedure depends on what you discovered.

A horse that responds to the direct rein, though slowly and reluctantly, and responds normally to leg aids can be ridden in the ring and on trails to practice turns without the neck rein. Try not to become frustrated. Add a little neck reining to help him along.

With young horses, trainers usually limit the initial training session to a few minutes, with a gradual increase of a few minutes each day. They don't want to injure unused muscles and tendons, and they don't want to frustrate the horse. A previously trained adult horse—especially one that's not being asked for a difficult new skill—can stay out for as long as his level of fitness permits.

Fully trained adult horses tend to get bored with repetitive and seemingly pointless action, so try to arrange reasons for your constant requests for the horse to turn. For example, direct him in a pattern at the walk, trot, or canter around barrels or cones, or ride along a trail that requires detours around trees or other barriers. This will help him accept his new method of reining.

Many of the Western horses that direct rein a little require a very wide rein to respond—a movement that's far too noticeable to look proper or to be comfortable for a rider. As you ride and turn, gradually bring the rein close to the horse's body until he accepts an unexaggerated, slight pressure as his signal.

A horse that neck reins exclusively will require a step-by-step changeover to his new style. Begin by neck-reining in his snaffle bridle. You will probably have to hold the reins in one hand for a few turns to give him the proper feel of reins on his neck. Then take the reins in different hands and add a wide and gentle direct rein to the turn. Your goal is to turn the horse with the neck rein while he feels the effect of the direct rein at the same time.

In responding to the unfamiliar direct rein, he may slow or stop, in which case you should continue to urge him forward as you ask for the turn. Or he may try to turn completely around. In this case, straighten him by reducing the direct rein pressure, adding neck rein on the side to which he is turning, or pulling very gently on the opposite side from his turn. You will have to adjust your rein cues depending on his degree of turn. When he turns in the direction you want, praise him and ease off on both the direct rein and the neck rein.

As you work on the combined reining, gradually lessen the amount of the neck rein and increase the amount of direct rein while keeping the leg aids consistent. With most horses, this will take just one session of riding; although, you may have to go through the process again the next time you ride to make sure that the horse remembers.

LEG AIDS

Use the proper leg aids as you turn even if your preliminary analysis shows that the horse did not respond to them. The combined signal of pressure on the girth, on the side to which he's turning, and pressure behind the girth, on the opposite side, has the natural effect of encouraging forward impulsion and a proper follow through of the hindquarters on the turn. The horse doesn't have to have been taught this in order to respond.

The rare Western horse that responds only to leg aids does not pose a problem, since you can ride him any style with no difficulty at all. But if you plan to advance him in English riding, add correct and very gentle direct reining to the leg aids as he makes his turns.

Because leg aids are enough for this horse, adding rein aids may give you too much turn. The feel of pressure on the side of his mouth may make him turn more than you want. In this case, straighten him out gently with the other rein. Do it consistently until he understands the amount of turn you are requesting according to the level of contact he feels in his mouth.

A well-trained Western horse that understands direct and neck reining will be a pleasure, particularly when you add the leg aids to the mix. You may be surprised at how much you can make him do with a slight pressure on or around the girth. Western horsemanship, with its tradition of riders' hands being occupied with ropes, guns, calves, or equipment, calls for a much looser rein than English riding. In a good Western horse most of the turns, pivots, slight changes of direction, sideways steps, and other actions can be accomplished with little use of the reins. Don't forget to include English-style direct reining as you work. You may be tempted to skip it altogether.

There are a few circumstances in which the leg aids are slightly different between Western and English riding. As mentioned before, rear-end collection at the halt is sometimes signaled to the Western horse with a slight squeeze just in front of the girth, while most English horses respond to the squeeze on or just behind the girth. Simply move your feet back slightly as you gently pull back. Say "Whoa" at the same time. Most horses seem to understand the concept, whether they have been taught the word or not.

Some Western horses, primarily cutting horses, can be turned with the touch of a heel on the shoulder, on the same side that the neck rein would be felt. It's not permitted in competition, but some are trained with this cue. You probably won't need to test for this cue with most Western-trained horses, but you may accidentally signal the horse and produce an unexpected turn if yours has been trained in cutting.

ADJUSTING PACE

Your Western-trained horse will probably be much too slow at the walk and canter for your English taste. The saddle is part of the reason. The Western saddle itself is much heavier and the center of balance further back. This extra weight behind tends to slow a horse down unless it's countered by a request for greater impulsion. The horse will be inclined to assume that his old pace will be the correct one, even when you make the change to the new saddle.

But the English hunt-type forward-seat saddle will by itself help encourage forward movement, both because your weight will be further forward and because you will be leaning slightly more forward. Both factors tend to encourage a faster pace. But even with the lighter, more forward saddle, the horse will still need greater impulsion, primarily with your legs.

As you urge with your legs, be especially careful of your contact with his mouth. He is probably used to pressure on his mouth as a signal to slow or stop, and the mere maintenance of contact during the early days of his retraining may confuse him about the pace you want. You may find it best to ride on a slightly looser rein than ideal in English riding as you retrain for a more forward pace.

A whip can be used too, but you must be careful not to punish the horse if he's going forward willingly, but just too slowly. He is not disobeying but instead is just doing what he has been asked to do in the past.

Picking up the pace was the most difficult task Judy Nixon faced in retraining Moja Matka into an English hunter after her successful career in Western pleasure, even though the mare was active and energetic. Signals had meant different things in her previous career.

"She had to learn to go forward," Nixon says. "It took four or five months to get her to use herself. At first, I tried a spur to ask her to go forward, but she would drop her head instead because as a Western horse she learned that the spur meant for her to do that. So I used a tap with the whip, and that got her to go off down the rail."

IMPROVING GAITS

Since she's an Arab, Moja Matka had no trouble with an energetic, evenly cadenced trot, but many other Western horses do. The problem is not that they are physically incapable of trotting well, but that Western riding doesn't lend itself to the gait. The so-called jog is not very comfortable in a Western saddle and is seldom used.

Your test ride may have shown you that your horse is naturally a good trotter and needs no corrective work, but you will still have to do a little training. Since he will not have done much trotting in his previous career as a Western horse, he should be introduced to trotting gradually, with limited periods at the gait during his early weeks of retraining.

During those periods pay close attention to your diagonals. If you are trotting in one direction only, alternate the diagonal on which you post. Though you would do this with any horse, do it more often than you would with a horse that is experienced at carrying a rider at the trot. If you are trotting around a ring, you rise when the horse's inside fore-leg is on the ground. Since you can't change that, alternate direction often, even as often as every other circuit, to avoid overstressing muscles and tendons. This will help him practice his turning aids too.

The Western horse may be a poor trotter that will require more work than this. A horse that trots too slowly or at an uneven pace is uncomfortable to ride in an English saddle, lacking enough momentum to help the rider post but being too irregular to comfortably sit.

The pace problem may be correctable by steady, strong urging, primarily of the legs. A steady squeeze, not lessened until the horse reaches and maintains the pace you want, may be enough to get a proper trot. If the procedure is repeated, the horse should learn the required pace of your desired trot and be able to reach and maintain it without constant urging.

An uneven gait may require some additional work. Poles laid on the ground can be helpful. They are widely used as a first step in training jumpers, but they can be extremely useful in developing the trot as well. When trotting poles are placed a few inches longer than a horse's normal stride, they encourage an extended trot.

But poles are equally useful in developing an even trot. The average 15-hand Quarter-type horse will have a stride of just over four feet at his moderate trotting pace. A series of poles placed that distance apart will force him, when he is trotted over them, to maintain strides of consistent length. That, with steady urging, should encourage an even gait. Extending the distance between the poles will encourage both extension and speed, but that should come after the horse learns to maintain a steady trot at a slower, more familiar speed, even without the poles to help.

The canter may also prove a difficult gait to maintain at an adequate English pace. Western horses often learn two running gaits. They are taught an extremely slow lope and a very quick gallop, with nothing in between. An English hunter-style rider usually wants a canter of moderate pace, rarely asking for anything faster or slower.

The Western-trained horse will probably go into his lope with a lessening of rein contact and normal leg aids, either pressure on or behind both sides of the girth to permit him to pick his own lead, or pressure behind the girth on the opposite side of the lead you want. Maintain good contact with the horse's mouth without yet restraining him. If the canter is fast enough, maintain the same level of contact and resume the leg aids if he shows signs of slowing.

If the pace is not sufficiently fast, urge more firmly, but make sure you don't noticeably lessen contact with the mouth. The horse may think you want a gallop, believing that there is no in-between running pace. Be prepared to keep him from a full gallop, while urging him faster than his little lope. It shouldn't take him long to understand that there is indeed a speed between the lope and the gallop.

CHANGING HEAD CARRIAGE

You will most likely want a higher head carriage and more vertical body shape than your horse used while he was being ridden Western. But you want the horse to flex his poll well and not raise his nose as much as he raises the rest of his head.

The snaffle bit that you are probably using as you begin to retrain should do much of the work for you. The jointed snaffle acts on the mouth differently than does the ported curb he used before. The snaffle, which bends downward on one or both sides with any kind of contact through the reins from the rider, places pressure on the bars, the lips, and the tongue. The horse, in a natural effort to escape the pressure, raises his head. The curb, with its cheek pieces causing even greater pressure on the tongue and its port pressing up on the roof of the mouth, causes a horse to try to escape the pressure by bringing his head into his chest and permitting his neck to bend.

For many horses, the action of the snaffle alone is enough to get the head and neck to a position desirable for English riding. Others raise their necks and heads properly but push their chins out. This isn't common with adult Western horses, since their experiences with the curb bit makes it an unlikely habit to have picked up.

Some do push out the chin as soon as they realize that the snaffle won't prevent it. These horses may require a dropped noseband or a martingale to maintain a perpendicular head while the neck comes up. A double bridle with a curb added to a snaffle can help.

If you want to stay with a simple snaffle and the horse persists in pushing his head and neck out, you will have to drive forward with firmly applied leg aids. At the same time, you usually have to put pressure on the bit to bring the chin in.

Occasionally stronger leg aids alone will bring the head up, since fast or extended gaits require the horse to carry his head higher in order to maintain balance. At a lazy, ambling gait the head can be lower without affecting balance, so make the horse move forward energetically.

Once the head and neck are at the desired height, you can work to get the flexion of the poll that you want for appearance and responsiveness. An Arab or Morgan trained for hunter-style riding will probably have more flex than will a short-necked Quarter Horse, but all horses should have some. The horse is urged to flex in the same way that he was as a Western horse, but you may be asking for more or less than he used to give. Urge forward with the legs, and give and take with the hands so that the horse maintains his pace but yields his jaw, bending at the poll while maintaining flexibility in the neck.

SHOEING

You probably had a visit from the farrier—presumably one familiar with shoeing English-style horses—before you began serious retraining. But you may find that you need an emergency visit during your program. A horse that had been used exclusively in Western pleasure will now be working harder than he had before.

Judy Nixon found that Moja Matka needed shoe pads to prevent soreness, since the horse had never been asked to cover ground in Western pleasure at the pace and extension that she was doing in English hunter. "She had been very laid back," Nixon says, "and now I was asking her to use herself and stride out. She was coming up sore, so I had to work a lot with her feet. We decided to go with pads."

Many Western-bred horses do tend to have relatively small feet for their body sizes, so you may find yours also needs some experimentation in trimming, shoeing, and perhaps pads. As with any sore horse, ease off until the cause of the soreness is discovered and the pain itself goes away. Foot problems should not be serious or long-term with a horse used on the flat, once he and his shoeing adjust to the new demands.

CHAPTER FIVE

English to Western

T RAINERS AND RIDERS CHANGE THEIR HORSES from English to Western style generally for the same reasons that they change them from English to Western. Most common is the simplest reason of all: it's their preferred style of riding. But there are other, more complicated reasons to change, including one that is exclusive to Western riding.

WHY CHANGE TO WESTERN?

A rider's desire to go Western may be based on something more important than simple preference. The Western seat is more secure. A very old, very young, inexperienced, nervous, or handicapped rider will find it easier to stay aboard a Western saddle than an English saddle. Such a rider may want to change back to English riding later, as his strength or confidence improves, but for the time being, Western is the safest way to go.

The horn of the Western saddle was originally intended to provide a means of attaching rope to the saddle. It is now used for that purpose only in roping events and in actual ranch use, but the horn remains an essential part of the saddle. Experienced riders rarely put a hand on the horn except perhaps to mount, but it's readily available for an insecure rider to grasp if he's afraid of slipping off.

In addition, the Western saddle has a built-up pommel in front and a high cantle in back, making it nearly impossible for a rider to slip off forward or backward. The stirrups are also easier for an unsteady rider to hold, since most Western stirrups feature a thicker and wider bottom bar than do English stirrups. Stirrup hoods, called tapaderos when used on Western saddles, are more common in Western riding than English. They, too, help keep the foot more securely where it belongs by preventing it from being pushed entirely through the stirrup.

The comparatively slow speed of the Western walk, jog, and lope also make the style safer for insecure riders. It's no mystery why public trail rides, no matter where the stable is located, usually feature Western trained horses.

The change to Western is also done by experienced horsemen who ride at a higher level. You may be thinking about it if your horse is a member of a breed that traditionally competes both ways, like Arabs

Morgans, like Arabs and several other breeds, can be shown Western as well as English.

and Morgans. He may be a member of a breed that has more recently added English events, like Quarter Horses, Paints, and Appaloosas, and you may want to expand both of your horizons.

The horse may be a member of a breed that normally doesn't go Western, like Thoroughbred, Standardbred, or one of the warmbloods, but you have him (or want to buy him) and you think that he will excel as a Western horse. He will be eligible for Western classes in all-breed shows, and he will be eligible for performance events in every competition except those exclusive to specific Western breeds.

Sometimes the choice is made by the horse's attitude and personality; sometimes it's made for conformation reasons. Arab trainer and competitor Judy Nixon believes that the former is more important. Assuming that a young Arab lacks the knee action to be a park horse, she decides on his future after initial breaking.

"I wait until I get on them," she says. "After the first couple of weeks, I make my decision based on their attitude. It's either a Western attitude or a hunter attitude, and that's the way I go."

A horse that is naturally slow and easygoing can certainly be urged into the quicker gaits of English riding. But he and his rider would undoubtedly be happier and ultimately more successful going Western even if he does learn to perform the gaits consistently.

Conformation plays a role in the decision to change to Western, too. A horse with a naturally low head carriage, a short neck, wide hindquarters, and hind legs set well underneath him will not only look better in Western tack, he also will have a better chance of reaching his potential as an athlete in the Western sports.

WHICH BREEDS WILL WORK?

Provided that he is sound and sane enough, any horse can be trained to be ridden Western, but some breeds prove to provide more likely prospects than others. The traditional Western breeds—Quarter Horse, Appaloosa, Paint, and other stock breeds—are obvious sources. But others produce good Western prospects too.

Almost every traditional English-style breed has individuals that better fit the Western horse ideal. American Saddlebreds that lack the extreme high head so prized in the breed can be allowed to drop and extend their necks. A Saddlebred that lacks the high action needed to show in his breed may still have the smooth gaits needed in a Western horse. If a Saddlebred's croup slopes more than the breed ideal, his hindquarters should still have the good rear-end impulsion and balance so prized in his own breed and in Western uses. Saddlebreds' size and shoulder makes them suitable for most Western events.

Western horsemen traditionally looked down on Thoroughbreds as being too tall, too light-boned, and too nervous to use with any success in Western activities. The stock breeds then proceeded to infuse Thoroughbred blood into their breeding programs in an effort to get a lot more speed and a little more height. As a result, a tall, light-boned, edgy horse no longer seems so unfamiliar or so undesirable.

At the same time, Thoroughbreds themselves are changing. Just as the Quarter Horse and other Western breed registries have encouraged the addition of Thoroughbred blood, Thoroughbred breeders have begun producing sturdier, more muscular horses for the shorter races that now dominate the Thoroughbred sport. These horses become available for retraining, either after or instead of racing.

In the case of the Thoroughbreds, no outside blood was introduced. Instead, nontraditional Thoroughbred types were selected in mating decisions. Because the vast majority of Thoroughbred races in North America are now sprints, the breeding industry has produced a horse with a shorter neck, shorter back, wider hindquarters, and less straight hock than the traditional, distance-running Thoroughbred. There are plenty of the old kind still around, since they are the ones that win Kentucky Derbies, but now most American Thoroughbreds are bred to run faster and more explosively over a shorter distance.

Because of the changes in each of the breeds, there are horses whose breed can't even be identified by experts. You may well find a properly registered Thoroughbred ideally conformed to be a Western riding or performance horse.

CONFORMATION PRECAUTIONS

Some conformation characteristics make Western riding difficult for certain horses. The horse's back has to be long enough to provide room for the larger Western saddle and the larger area over which the rider's weight is carried. But the greater weight of the saddle plus the fact that the center of balance is further back than in English riding makes a long-backed horse vulnerable to injury. A horse that has an extremely long back but does not have much muscling on either side of the spine might not stay sound under a Western saddle.

A horse with a natural crest to the neck may never be able to get the flat topline and low head carriage desirable in some kinds of Western riding. This may not matter to you if your plans don't include showing or competition.

EQUIPMENT

Before you ride, decide on the equipment you plan to use. Your choices can affect the comfort of both you and your horse and the ease with which he retrains.

SADDLES

Most Western riders choose their saddles according to the activities they plan for the horse, as well as for their own riding comfort. These are both legitimate factors to consider, but for a horse coming out of an English saddle, you must also consider his comfort.

First decide whether you want to use a single- or double-rigged saddle. Single rigging means that a single cinch connects the saddle to the horse. Double rigging (you'll sometimes hear it referred to as full rigging) features two cinches, one just behind the elbow and another several inches back towards the flank.

Double rigging is certainly more secure, and it's popular in Western sports that might cause a saddle to slip. Roping horses are usually double rigged, as are barrel horses. It's usually unnecessary in pleasure or trail riding. In a double-rigged saddle, the front cinch fits very close to the elbow. A straight or short shoulder often rubs the cinch, and a horse that has never experienced a girth in that spot can suffer injury and infection to an untoughened area of skin.

Single rigging features a cinch that fits just about where an English girth does, although Western saddle design features several variations of ring placement that can bring the cinch closer to or further from the elbow. But almost any single-rigged saddle makes a straight-shouldered horse safer from chafing.

Double rigging does prevent the saddle from slipping back on a horse with high withers, and you might find this necessary with some English-style breeds. Be sure to introduce the second cinch carefully, since few horses like the idea of straps so close to their flanks. If the high-withered horse simply does not accept the flank cinch, try a single-rigged saddle with a strong breast collar to help keep the saddle from slipping back.

Riders usually choose the height of the pommel and cantle according to how securely they wish to be held in the saddle. But height front and back can also affect where the horse is going to have to carry your weight, and this is a necessary consideration for a horse used to carrying weight forward.

A high pommel in front will invariably push a rider's weight backward (behind the horse's natural center of balance). This problem is compounded with a comfortably stuffed and built up front of the seat. This also slides the rider's weight backward. A horse ridden English style will have developed the muscles in the shoulders and the front section of the back to handle the weight there. His muscles will not be ready to handle weight further back. Discomfort and possible permanent injury may result.

If you can't find a saddle with a flatter front, introduce the horse to the backward-sloping saddle gradually, allowing his muscles time to develop. This is particularly true if you and the saddle you are using are heavy.

A synthetic saddle may be the answer to the weight problem for some horses being retrained out of English tack. The synthetics are lighter to begin with—about half the weight of leather saddles—and they feature seats that can be well padded without being built up in front.

Saddle fitting is another consideration for an English-trained horse. The average Western saddle will fit a greater variety of horses than the average English saddle, since they are usually built a little wider for stock-horse backs and withers. A too-wide saddle can be fitted to the individual horse with one or more pads. You can also find wider-than-average Western saddles, described as having "semi–Quarter Horse" or "full–Quarter Horse" trees. One of these will almost certainly fit any English-trained horse that you bring to Western riding.

All Western saddles are used with blankets or pads anyway, but use more than you think you need during your early weeks of retraining. A Western saddle has many more pressure spots than an English saddle, and your horse will need extra protection from chafing as his skin toughens up in new spots.

In the past, your choice of a cinch would have been limited. Mohair cord cinches were the rule, and they are still the most common. But you can find felt-lined nylon cinches, webbing cinches, and various cinches made of synthetic materials. Start with the cinch most like the one used on the horse's English tack for the easiest transition.

BRIDLES

You may certainly continue using your English-trained horse's familiar bridle when you ride him Western style in a Western saddle. There is no Western sport or activity that can't be done well with a simple English headstall and noseband buckled to a plain snaffle bit, provided the horse is capable of being handled in a mild bit. Your horse won't be the only Western horse around with such headgear. Snaffle bridles are becoming increasingly common in Western riding.

A horse that wears a double bridle or pelham while going English can continue to wear these too; although, he may be the only one around that does. There is nothing about the way these bridles control and direct a horse that would make them unsuitable for most kinds of Western activities.

There's one exception to this: most breed shows require the use of a Western curb bit on any horse over the age of five in Western classes. If your English-trained horse is a member of one of the breeds with such a restriction and you intend to show, you will have to move to a curb. Check your breed rules to find out what's required in terms of headstall, reins, and bit.

You will also want to change to a curb if a traditional Western appearance is important to you. No matter how many Western horses begin their training in snaffles, and no matter how well they go in them, many Western horsemen think that a big ring on the side of the mouth just doesn't look right.

If you don't have to move to a curb, think carefully before doing so. The regular Western curb is considered more severe than the jointed snaffle for two main reasons. The first is that the curb usually features a port—a U-shaped bend in the middle of the bar of the mouthpiece. A low port presses on the tongue more than the snaffle does when the reins are pulled back. A high port presses on both the tongue and the roof of the mouth. This can be very painful if the pull is sudden or strong.

The other reason for the curb's potential severity is that it includes shanks—pieces of metal that extend above and below the mouthpiece. The shanks, called cheeks in Western riding, add extra leverage to the pull, increasing the effect of the mouthpiece and the port. The longer the cheeks, the more severe the effect.

The combination of port and cheek provide so much pressure in the center of the mouth, regardless of whether one or both reins are pulled, that it is not a good bit with which to teach an English-trained horse to neck rein. As you'll see later, this part of retraining must sometimes be done with combined rein signals. Direct reining with a curb causes pain or even injury, neither of which contributes to a pleasant retraining experience for the horse.

If and when you do move on to the curb, note that English and Western curb straps differ. Both connect the sides of the curb under the horse's chin. Traditionally, the English strap was a chain that hooked onto the curb bit on a double bridle, while the Western one was leather.

Today, some Western curb straps have chain in the middle, but they still have leather tabs that buckle rather than hook. Both increase the effect of the curb bit, but remember that English riders using a double bridle are able to choose to use the snaffle bit. Your English-trained horse may have only rarely experienced the tightening of a curb chain as it came into play.

Just as English riders are able to choose from bits that combine the mild effects of the snaffle and the more severe effects of the curb, Western riders can now do the same. One of these bits might be a good choice for a horse moving from English to Western. One possibility is the long-cheeked snaffle, sometimes called the Western snaffle or the cowboy snaffle. This bit features the jointed mouth of the ringed snaffle, along with the cheeks of the curb. It's more severe than the snaffle because of the leverage provided by the cheeks, but it lacks the pressure on the tongue and roof of the mouth caused by the ported curb and is much milder. It resembles a regular Western curb when it's in the horse's mouth.

You will also find shanked gag bits in Western tack shops. The gag, made popular by polo players, moves in the horse's mouth by means of a round cheek strap that travels through two holes on each side of the mouth. The effect is to give the horse warning that the curb action of the bit is about to come into play. It allows the horse to do what the rider has requested or to correct an improper action before the curb tells him he must do it.

The gag is not common in Western riding because it tends to encourage a higher head carriage, but there are some horses and some situations in which it proves useful. You rarely see gags in competitions, but some Western trainers use them in schooling as a step beyond the snaffle for young horses. The gag may also serve that function for your older, English-trained horse.

You may also alternate bits. Judy Nixon not only breaks both Western and hunter horses with snaffles, she continues training both with snaffles after they have learned their show bits. "In Western pleasure, I always work them with a snaffle bit. One or two days before a show, I'll drop my hands and neck rein, but they're always schooled with two hands," Nixon says.

Other trainers also find it safer and more thorough to school with the direct-reined snaffle. They limit the use of the curb to situations in which it's needed or required.

The headstall itself makes little difference. As an English horse, yours will have worn a throatlatch and browband on his headstall, and he probably will have worn a separate noseband. If you retain the snaffle, you will need the browband and throatlatch, but the noseband will be optional unless you plan to add a martingale. If you like a more Western look but still want a mild ringed snaffle, try leaving the noseband off. The headstall will show off the face nicely, but you'll be able to keep the horse's familiar bit.

MARTINGALES AND TIE-DOWNS

Martingales are used less often in Western riding than English, but a horse that needs one to keep his head down while going English will probably need one going Western too, since desirable head carriage in Western riding is lower than in English riding. There is the possibility that he tossed his head or stretched his neck going English because his tack was uncomfortable. Try him in the tack you plan for him before you make a decision about a martingale.

The martingale that's most often used in Western riding is the tie-down—a kind of standing martingale that fastens from a separate cable noseband to the cinch. In addition to preventing stargazing and head tossing, it helps prevent rearing. It also helps the horse understand a signal to stop and turn on his haunches, so it's regular equipment for ropers and some barrel racers. It's not permitted in several kinds of Western showing, and it rarely has a place in casual Western riding.

Less familiar to Western riders, but potentially more useful, is the English-style running martingale. It may prove particularly useful for English-trained horses trying to learn the headset necessary for Western riding. Unlike the tie-down, the running martingale is almost always used with a snaffle bit, so it's easier on the mouth. The Y-shaped straps of the running martingale travel through rings placed on each rein, with the single center strap attaching to the girth through a light breast collar. The running martingale limits head tossing and stargazing like the standing martingale does, but it allows the horse more flexibility of movement in his neck and shoulders.

Some Western trainers also use draw reins to train young horses to flex their necks while keeping their necks and heads low. Draw reins travel from the hands through the snaffle rings and back to the girth and are usually well accepted by older horses that have learned their basics English style. Since draw reins are somewhat more common in English training, your horse may have already experienced them.

Judy Nixon uses draw reins on horses that need their head carriage adjusted to go Western. She also believes in the so-called Arab martingale, which is one of several designs that feature rings nearer to the shoulder. These help control the level of the neck and shoulder in addition to the head. An increasing number of Western trainers also use a rediscovered European martingale, sometimes called a German martingale, which features D-rings on the reins so you can select the level of control and thereby the headset.

Ideally, your horse will lower his head and neck through appropriate training, but equipment is available if you need it. Since less is best for any horse, start with the simplest combination of equipment possible, then add only if you find you need mechanical help.

THE TEST RIDE

For your initial ride, use a snaffle bridle with the lightest, most evenly balanced single-rigged saddle you can find. The saddle is not as important as the bridle for this first ride, since you will probably spend only a few minutes checking your horse's previous level of training.

MOUNTING AND MOVING OUT

As discussed in Chapter Four, there are minor differences in the most common methods of mounting English and Western. Most English riders face the rear before swinging aboard, while most Western riders face the horse's side. Each method is an acceptable alternative to the other style, and it doesn't matter to most horses how you choose to climb aboard.

If you tend to grasp the horn with your right hand in order to pull yourself aboard (an acceptable but sometimes undesirable technique), be sure that the saddle fits properly and is going to remain in place. A wide-tree saddle on a Thoroughbred-type horse with high and narrow withers may slip sideways if a rider pulls on the horn.

English and Western horses usually start with the same leg aids. Slight pressure on the horse's sides, usually on the girth, should prompt him to move out. The English-trained horse will expect more contact with his mouth than a Western rider is inclined to offer him. Since you will be using a snaffle, take up the reins just enough so that you can feel the bit. The horse won't mind a loose, Western-style rein, but he may give you an inaccurate idea of his willingness, his preferred paces, and the speed of his responses to your cues.

THE AIDS

After the horse moves comfortably forward for a few steps, you may begin to test the aids. The first thing you'll want to discover is the horse's responsiveness to neck reining. Loosen the reins enough to prevent any chance of accidental direct reining, and perform a proper neck rein for a simple turn. Do it several times. Try turns in each direction, some with leg aids and some without. Judge whether the horse knows what to do, whether he responds slowly and with confusion or doesn't respond at all. If he does appear to neck rein, make sure it's the rein signal he's following and not just the leg aids or the weight of your body or any accidental verbal signals you may be giving.

You may be pleasantly surprised by how much your English-trained horse understands about neck reining. A horse trained to a high level (or ridden by a skilled English rider) will have learned to respond to an indirect rein on the opposite side of the neck from his turns. It's applied in English riding to adjust the arc of turns, among other uses. While the horse may miss the simplicity of the direct rein, he may understand the objective and respond to your requests. It may be a little slow at first, but your satisfaction with his responses will quickly teach him that he's right. A horse must understand neck reining to perform adequately in any kind of Western riding.

You have already checked response to the leg aids for starting and turning, so a further test may include the aids for the correct lead at the lope. Again, English and Western trainers usually teach the horse to take a particular lead in response to pressure behind the girth on the opposite side from the required lead. Some turn the head slightly to the opposite side. In both styles, some trainers prefer that horses learn to accept the lead with their heads kept perfectly straight. The higher the level reached by the horse in his previous career, the more likely you will be able to keep the head straight while requesting a lead.

The advanced English horse will have learned the flying change of lead, in which the rider asks for the change during the canter or gallop. Advanced Western horses do it too, but they are usually trained to do a flying change on a figure eight or serpentine, not a straightaway. Ask the horse the way you would a Western horse, giving the leg cues for a change and shifting your weight to the inside at the point where his hind legs are down. Since it's harder to do a flying change on a straight-away, an English-trained horse that can do it at all should be able to do it in a Western-style figure eight or serpentine.

HEAD CARRIAGE

During a test ride with a snaffle bit, you may not be able to check for the kind of head carriage that you'll be able to obtain once you change him to a curb bit. But you should be able to determine the horse's pref-erence in head carriage once you drop your hands and give up steady contact with his mouth. Try a loose rein for a few minutes to see what he does with his head when he has less bit contact.

You may have already noticed the horse's head go down as you checked for his response to neck reining; if it didn't then, and still doesn't as you ride with a loose rein, decide if head carriage matters. For casual riding and some performance events, a high head is insignificant. For Western pleasure classes, it's impossible. For Western riding and trail-horse competitions, judges will not grade down a head carried at a moderate height, a carriage typical of many English-type breeds.

A horse destined for Western pleasure competition will have to work to lower the head while maintaining a flexed poll. Plan your retraining program accordingly.

PACE AND ATTITUDE

Most Western activities call for a quiet, easy-going attitude and a slow pace at all gaits except the gallop. Liveliness is not appreciated for its own sake. Even the performance events expect horses to be calm and quiet except when they burst into action during their events.

Since English sports tend to encourage strong, fast gaits and energetic performance, your English-trained horse will probably move out faster than you want. See if a lessening of the leg aids is enough to slow him down to the correct Western pace at each gait. If not, a change in attitude will become part of his retraining.

No well-trained horse should react excessively to outside distractions, but Western horses are supposed to be oblivious. See how your horse responds to unfamiliar sights and sounds that come from somewhere other than you. A too-responsive horse should quiet down as part of his retraining for pace and attitude.

OTHER SKILLS

You may check the horse for a few other Western skills. A horse previously trained English will almost certainly not understand your requests, but try them anyway on the chance that he learned them prior to his English career.

With a horse that you've determined is controllable and steady, you can find out if he can do a sliding stop, or at least a sudden stop with his hindquarters pulled well underneath him. At a gallop or very fast canter, signal the horse to stop by sitting well down and very slightly back in the saddle. Pull back lightly with the reins, while lifting your hands. The cues won't be precisely correct with a snaffle, but you may get an idea of the horse's talents.

You may also check to see if the horse knows how to ground tie, provided you're confident the horse is not going to run off. Get off, pull the reins over the horse's head, unbuckle the rein ends, and let the ends drop to the ground in front of the horse. A horse that stands still is either very lazy or knows how to ground tie.

A horse that knows these specialized Western skills has undoubtedly been trained Western at some point in the past. Even if his other Western skills were rusty, you will probably have little work ahead of you to remake him into a Western horse. Other horses will require a little more work.

THE RETRAINING PROGRAM

Depending on what you discovered during your test ride, you may begin retraining in either a simple ringed snaffle, a jointed mouth curb, or the Western curb you plan to use on the horse once he's fully retrained. The horse that didn't respond to neck reining at all should remain in a snaffle. One that understands the concept at all can be retrained in the Western snaffle or a carefully used curb.

NECK REINING

A horse will never look or act like a Western horse unless he knows how to neck rein, so that must be the first goal in your retraining program. The following procedure assumes that the horse doesn't neck rein at all. If yours does—but poorly—you may follow the steps exactly to reinforce and sharpen his knowledge. Otherwise, skip to the second step.

In either case, the change to neck reining shouldn't take long. Even to a direct rein–trained horse, the concept of moving in the opposite direction from the rein is easy to grasp. It's natural for a horse to move away from pressure. Leg aids work on that principle, and the horse will learn quickly to associate moving away from a leg aid applied on the same side as the rein. To teach neck reining, you can use either a Western or English saddle.

Move out on your first training ride from a spot that will allow you and the horse to move for a few moments without having to turn.

You want to be comfortable with each other before beginning the potentially difficult demands.

Whether you start along the rail or on the center line of a ring depends upon the horse. A horse that stays close to the rail without urging will learn well along the outside of a ring, but one that cuts corners or constantly moves to the center will require urging to stay on the rail, which may conflict with your turn signals. Until you are sure what kind of horse you have, you may find it easier to work along a straight line in the center of the ring.

As you work on the first step of neck-rein training, you will ride with two hands, one on each rein. Bring the reins into your grasp through the bottom of your hand, English style. You will be using direct reins during the first two steps of retraining.

Begin to teach neck reining with two hands on the reins. This is most familiar and comfortable for the horse.

In fact, you may continue using the reins in the little-finger grasp even after your horse is fully retrained to neck reining and you're using the typical one-handed Western style. The style is acceptable in most Western activities, although it's somewhat less common than the method of bringing the reins into the hands from the top, next to the thumbs.

Begin a series of turns using the normal leg aids of pressure behind the girth on the opposite side from the turn, plus a little pressure on the girth on the inside, if needed for impulsion. Use the direct-rein signal by pulling lightly on the rein on the side of the turn.

The English-trained horse will turn on this signal alone, but as you give the expected signal, bring the opposite rein across the neck. Be careful not to pull on the mouth on that side. You want the horse to feel the presence of the neck rein as he responds to his normal turn signal.

*The horse is feeling his familiar direct
rein, but he is experiencing the neck
rein at the same time.*

*Switch to an English-style flat hand
when you first use single-hand reining.*

Be sure to change the direction of the turn often. Also, vary the number of strides between the requests to turn to make sure he isn't performing automatically rather than paying attention to the commands.

The number of turns you make depends on how much the horse already understands about neck training, how patient he is, and how comfortable he is likely to be in his new saddle. A horse that seemed to know a little about neck reining during your test ride might require only a dozen turns with double-rein signals. One that knew nothing will probably need many times that, possibly spread over several schooling sessions.

Your next step is to change from two-hand to one-hand riding. The English method of holding one rein calls for a flat hand, with one rein coming through next to the little finger and the other entering between the thumb and the forefinger. The reins cross under the face-down palm. This can be done with either hand and allows direct reining in either direction; although it's a little easier to turn left if you hold the reins in the left hand, and likewise with the right.

Continue your double signals with one flat, English-style hand. The one hand lessens the pull on the direct rein and tends to cause the other rein to lie on the neck. With this step, the horse begins to get used to a rider using one hand to neck rein while still receiving double signals. If you want your horse to get used to the proper single hand from the beginning, use your left hand only during this step.

Continue your double-rein signals along with normal leg aids for a dozen or more turns, again being careful not to accidentally pull on the

By the time you change to Western-style single-hand reining, the horse should be fully familiar with neck reining.

bit on the opposite side of the turn. If you have chosen to use your left hand only, you may find your wrist isn't strong enough to direct rein properly in each direction with the reins in just one hand. Change the reins to the hand on the side of the turn just before you ask for the turn.

Once you believe the horse has understood the fact that he is receiving two-rein signals to turn, begin to lessen the direct-rein pressure while maintaining or even slightly exaggerating the neck rein and the leg aids. Before long, the horse should be able to turn with the direct rein omitted altogether. You may have to continue exaggerating the neck rein and the leg aids for a while, but you should be able to return to aids of normal intensity within a short period of time.

As soon as the horse responds to the neck rein every time you ask for a turn, move him on to the final bit you plan to use. Continue working on neck-reined turns with the new bit, but don't be tempted to reinforce a poor or slow turn with a direct rein on a curb bit. Instead, apply stronger leg aids. A horse that makes a lot of mistakes should be returned to a snaffle and trained again with double-rein signals.

HEAD CARRIAGE

There is a trend in Western riding to move away from the extreme low head carriage that has been the rule in the show ring and, to a lesser extent, in casual riding. The activity that requires the lowest head, Quarter Horse Western pleasure, now has a standard calling for a poll no lower than the top of the withers. Other Western riding events only call for relaxed and natural head carriage.

Nevertheless, Western judges, trainers, and riders have a specific idea of what's relaxed and natural, and it's not a high head. An English-trained horse destined for Western showing will probably have to learn a lower head carriage.

Some English-type breeds, such as Thoroughbreds and some warmbloods, do tend to have low heads and may need nothing more than a change of attitude and a minor change of equipment. Others may need more work.

"The head usually comes down naturally with the bigger bit," Judy Nixon points out. "The curb weighs enough more."

It's not just bit weight that helps head carriage. The action of the curb against the roof of the mouth also discourages the lifting of the head, so a switch to a curb bit may be enough to obtain the head height you want.

As mentioned before, martingales and draw reins can also encourage lower head carriage. Except for the tie-downs used in roping and speed events, they are almost never used in other Western competitions or casual riding. But these devices are widely used by trainers while schooling all kinds of Western horses.

A few horses maintain a high head in spite of the curb or schooling with a martingale. But even they may improve once they master the next step in Western retraining.

PACE AND ATTITUDE

Just as desirable as a low head in Western riding is a relaxed attitude. Along with an easy-going attitude should come slow and comfortable gaits. Most English-trained horses will have spent their working lives being urged to go forward, to move out quickly at all gaits, and to be lively. Most will be too fast for many kinds of Western riding.

Some of the previous retraining steps may have already served to slow your horse. A move from the snaffle to the more severe curb may have done it. The lowering of the head may have helped, too, especially if the horse had been urged to carry an unnaturally high head while going English. The return to a more comfortable head carriage may serve to calm him and reduce tension.

The use of the reins also plays a role. Both tradition and the curb bit require a much looser rein than the English-trained horse is accustomed to feeling. Expectations to the contrary, loosening your grip will rarely prompt a horse to go faster, unless you increase your leg aids at the same time. Looser reins tend to relax a horse. This may help slow his pace and calm his demeanor.

If these steps are insufficient, there are other options to explore. Before you try any of them, make sure your leg cues are light and used only when necessary. Once the horse responds to the leg by going forward or performing another requested action, stop the leg pressure immediately. Resume leg aids only if he stops altogether or begins to move in the wrong direction.

Your first option is the most obvious. Try give-and-take with the reins. "I'll take back until the horse slows," Judy Nixon says, "but then I let go immediately." She will repeat this process as often as necessary. Remember that the pull has to be light because you are trying to adjust pace, not stop the horse.

"If taking back doesn't do it, I'll try moving off the rail," Nixon says. "I'll go in small circles. Once he slows, I'll move back to the rail and go on." Circling forces the horse to take more careful—and slower—steps. The correct pace is rewarded by a lessening of aids.

Stopping the forward momentum of a too-fast pace also works. "I'll stop the horse and back up a few steps," Nixon says. "Then I'll go forward." This helps break the horse's mental habit of thinking that all movement should be quick.

STOPPING

Several Western performance events require a sliding stop. Western pleasure and casual riding do not, although all Western riding activities value a good stop in which the horse gets his hindquarters well underneath him.

An English-trained horse may not stop well enough for Western uses. If yours doesn't, work on a normal collected stop, exaggerating the cues slightly. Take back with the reins, as lightly as you can while still prompting the stop, and squeeze with both legs. The leg aids urge the hindquarters forward and under while the rein pressure stops the front end from continuing forward.

An English-trained horse may or may not entirely understand the word "Whoa," but you should use it during retraining. The verbal cue will be useful to a horse that has never learned a collected stop. Otherwise, he may be confused by the leg pressure.

A horse destined for Western performance events may have to be taught the sliding stop. For suggestions, see Chapter Ten.

GROUND TYING

Ground tying is a useful skill for any Western horse. Horses usually learn to ground tie as young animals, but there's no reason an older, English-trained horse can't learn it.

Choose an enclosed space, one small enough for you to be able to catch the horse if he runs, but not so small that the horse will stand still whether he is held or not.

Attach a long lead rope to the halter. Stand the horse, allowing the lead rope to droop down to the ground in front of his forefeet while you hold the end. Be prepared to take up the slack or drop your end if the horse becomes restive. You don't want him to become tangled in the rope.

At first, stand just a few feet in front of the horse, holding the end of the rope in your hands. If the horse moves, try to keep him in place by saying "Whoa!" Return to him to set him up again if necessary.

Gradually move further away, allowing more of the lead rope to lie on the ground. When he stands consistently, drop your end of the rope altogether. Move further and further away, stopping the horse with your voice if necessary. When you believe that the horse is ready, try leaving the ring. Stay within sight and voice range at first, then move out of sight.

The ground-tying program should be spread over a number of training sessions, since few horses can be expected to stand for more than a few minutes at a time. Some horses will learn to ground tie quickly and easily, while others never learn at all. Most should be able to learn to stand for short periods with the rider nearby but not attached—even this is useful.

PART THREE

Riding and Driving

CHAPTER SIX

Driving to Riding

UNTIL THE TWENTIETH CENTURY, HORSEMEN FREQUENTLY faced the task of turning a driving horse into a riding animal. Harness horses were more common and certainly more useful than saddle horses, and all horses except those bred specifically for saddle were likely to receive their initial training under harness.

Still, plenty of horses were needed for riding, and a horse that changed hands during his lifetime was probably going to have to learn to be ridden. He usually did learn, quickly and successfully, and the accomplishment was not considered to be anything remarkable.

Times have changed, however, and many people today have great misgivings about the prospect of teaching a harness-trained horse to be ridden. They believe—and rightly so—that it's unnatural for a prey animal like a horse to accept another animal on his back. The antipathy to being ridden can be overcome in an open-minded young horse, but some horsemen think the natural fear may be too firmly fixed in an adult. What's more, they think, there is no huge population of harness horses available for retraining, since driving animals make up only a small fraction of the modern horse population.

The truth is that horses that already know how to be driven are usually no more difficult to train to ride than are young, untrained horses, regardless of age. In fact, most driving horses can be taught to carry a rider much more quickly and far more easily than can unbroken horses.

It is true that there aren't as many harness horses as riding horses in the overall horse population, but among them are some of the best-natured, most intelligent, and most useful animals in the world.

Moreover, as long as horse people fear the retraining and believe they can't do it, those horses can be available at reasonable prices.

WHERE TO FIND PROSPECTS

Likely subjects for retraining usually come from three categories: working draft horses, animals bred or trained to compete in driving sports, and harness racehorses. There are advantages and disadvantages to each group in your search for a prospect.

WORKING DRAFT BREEDS

Since there is no practical reason in the modern world to use a driving horse for farm labor or transportation, there are very few draft horses being bred in North America strictly for labor. A number of people maintain draft breeds just for the love of the breed, while companies often use the offspring of their breeding stock for entertainment, advertising, and education. Occasionally, some of these horses become available if the company that owns them decides to cull its herd. Others may be bought for harness work by an owner who later decides that a riding horse would be more useful. Some are intended for double duty all along but were trained for harness first.

Doc and Prince were well into their harness careers before anybody thought of riding them. The two Suffolks are used for carriage driving, hayrides, and other events requiring a strong and handsome matched pair. They were purchased by David and Kathleen Bradham to join a pair of Belgians in their carriage business.

They did the job well. So why train them to ride?

"I had people who wanted to ride," Dave Bradham says. "I'd trained the Belgians, so I thought I'd try with the Suffolks."

The Bradhams acquired Prince and Doc for their business, but you can shop for a harness horse specifically to retrain. You can find draft horses suitable for retraining in many of the same places you can find riding horses. The horses may be advertised in local newspapers or regional equine publications; although some owners rely on word of mouth to find new owners for their culls. The sellers, often organizations or businesses, will probably be honest with you about why they are getting rid of a particular horse. If they don't volunteer the information, ask. You don't want to try to retrain a horse that's being sold because he likes to bite the customers. You do want to consider a horse that doesn't make the cut because he's a little too small. After all, a small Clydesdale makes a better riding prospect than a big one.

DRIVING-SPORT FAILURES

Horses bred or trained to compete in driving sports sometimes fail at those sports. Occasionally, the rejects haven't even failed, and they are sold at prices far below what a healthy, well-conformed, well-behaved horse should bring.

Much driving competition involves pairs, and an oddly colored horse rarely matches another. Even in singles competition, drivers tend to believe that their horses will be marked down for unusual white markings or an odd body color.

Size matters, too. A horse who doesn't quite match his teammates in height or build, or one who's a little too big or a little too small for the common competition categories, may fail at competition driving regardless of his pulling talents.

Horses who are poorly conformed for driving sports tend to be great bargains if they are members of breeds closely identified with driving. Morgans and Saddlebreds who fail at driving have other options within their breeds. Others, like Hackneys, are used mostly for driving. A driving-sport horse who lacks brilliant action or who has insufficient shoulder strength to pull should have been a riding horse from the beginning. These horses may become available at bargain prices. See Chapter Two for suggestions on how to locate driving horses.

RACEHORSES

The largest single category of prospects to retrain for riding is made up of harness racehorses who are too slow or too old to race. In North

America these will be Standardbreds. There are other harness racing breeds, primarily the Russian and French Trotters, but you almost certainly won't find them outside of Russia or France.

It's hard to say how many of these animals become available each year. The annual Standardbred foal crop in North America hovers around 10,000, and the average life expectancy of a Standardbred is about twenty years. Since they are not permitted to race past the age of fourteen (very few race even that long), you can presume that tens of thousands of them face a life other than racing each year.

The minority go to breeding farms or to retirement with their owners. The rest are sold, some to Amish farmers, some to pleasure driving homes. Many go to meat packers.

Almost all can be trained to ride. In France, there is even a well-organized program to race trotters under saddle, with more than $2 million available in purses for ridden trotters each year.

Prospects obtained from the racetrack are more likely to be unsound than other retraining prospects, but the meaning of *sound* differs depending upon whether the horse will be used for racing or pleasure riding. The main office of a local racetrack may direct you to a source for a retired Standardbred or to an organization that works to place them.

The United States Trotting Association, the breed registry for Standardbreds, has begun to actively encourage retraining of harness racers after their track careers. The USTA sponsors the Standardbred Equestrian Program. They will be able to give you information on Standardbreds, where to find them, and what you can do with them. Contact the USTA at 750 Michigan Avenue, Columbus, Ohio 43215; 614/224-2291.

Sometimes prospects for retraining come right off the breeding farm or from breeding-stock sales. Some of these horses have physical characteristics that make them unsuitable for training or breeding—often poor leg conformation—which suggests that they or their offspring won't stay sound through race training. However, they may be fine for training to ride.

If you live near a farm, you can call and ask if they are looking to cull a mare. One who can't produce salable foals will probably cost you less than $1,000—sometimes much less. They will be fully vaccinated and well cared for.

THE PACING QUESTION

There is one important consideration if your retraining prospect happens to be a Standardbred, whether he has raced or not. There is a chance that the gait he uses when you ask him to go faster than a walk will not be a trot. He will pace instead.

Instead of legs at the opposite corners moving forward at the same time, the two legs on each side work in tandem. Among other domesticated animals, only camels and a few breeds of dogs are known to pace by preference.

How big a chance do you have of getting a pacer if you acquire a Standardbred? A substantial one; although statistics are misleading. Four out of five Standardbreds who set foot on the racetrack in North America pace rather than trot. Pacing is more popular for bettors, trainers, and drivers, because it's slightly faster and somewhat more consistent. Consequently, the majority of modern Standardbreds are bred and trained to pace.

The pace is not the usual gait for a riding horse, and if your prospect paces, you are probably going to think about teaching him to trot instead. The change is not always easily made, but it can be done. The following explains how.

DISCOVER HIS TRUE GAIT

First, find out if he really paces. The horse may have impeccable pacing bloodlines, and he may have started a hundred pacing races, but, given a choice, he may trot rather than pace.

Many pacers are natural trotters who are taught the faster gait and then encouraged to maintain it under harness by the use of hobbles. These are loops attached to the harness that make it impossible for the horse to maintain a trot at speed.

Before you worry about teaching your pacer to trot, lead him as you run alongside. See what gait he chooses. You may already have a horse who trots everywhere except under harness on the racetrack.

If he paces and he's recently out of training, give him time before you decide that he's a natural pacer. Turn him out for a few days and try again.

DECIDE IF IT MATTERS

If he hasn't turned himself into a trotter after a few days in the pasture, there is one additional step to take before you begin his gait conversion. Decide if you can live with a pacer. People do, and they have for thousands of years. Even though the pace has to be taught to some Standardbreds and artificially maintained in many more, it is not an unnatural gait for the horse.

The tendency to pace exists somewhere in the equine gene pool. Trotting has always been more prevalent than pacing, but descriptions and art tell us that pacers have existed and have been used for riding for centuries. The earliest illustrations of the *Canterbury Tales* show several of Chaucer's pilgrims mounted on pacers. Legend has it that Paul Revere completed his midnight ride aboard a Narragansett Pacer, a now extinct breed that provided some of the foundation blood for the modern Standardbred.

The bottom line is this: You can ride a pacer, and you will probably find it comfortable. You and your horse will look different from the others in the trail ride, though. If you want to look like everybody else, you can try to change your pacer's natural gait.

SHOEING

Your first step is to consult a farrier, preferably one who has worked with Standardbreds. A farrier experienced with other gaited breeds might also have worthwhile suggestions. Just remember that a farrier who has trimmed and shod Standardbreds to change gaits will probably have done the opposite of what you want. He or she will most likely have been asked to help develop the more lucrative pace in a horse that preferred to trot.

The farrier will probably advise adding weight to the front shoes, either heavier shoes or toe weights on normal-weight shoes. The amount of weight depends on the horse's size, feet, and cannon bone, but it should start with a few ounces. The trainer of a nineteenth-century trotting star named Snuggler wrote that he put two-pound shoes on each of the horse's front feet to convert him from the then-unwanted pace to the trot. That story seems unlikely, but Snuggler probably did use much heavier than the normal six-ounce harness-racing shoes in front.

After adding toe weights, try the horse on a lunge line. Most Standardbreds are trained to lunge very early in their lives, since they are first put under harness about the time of their chronological first birthdays. You will almost certainly have no trouble using the lunge line to test and develop the gait.

SMALL CIRCLES

The addition of toe weights may be enough to prompt the trot. If not, here's something else to try on the lunge line. The smaller the circle he's asked to make, the more difficult it is for a four-legged animal to maintain a pacing gait. Lungeing a horse in increasingly smaller circles will probably force him to trot. You must be careful, since there may be a horse so determined to pace that he will fall down rather than trot. But most will use the gait that will get him around the circle that he's asked to complete.

After he trots on the turn, lengthen the distance between turns, keeping a consistent speed so that he can't return to a pace. He won't be able to reach a pace out of a trot without slowing to a walk or to a stop, or hopping. If you don't let him do any of those things, you will be able to keep him on the trot. Gradually lengthen the straight distances until he can trot consistently for several minutes.

Remember to change directions regularly. As in all lungeing, changing direction is important to maintain soundness and to develop proportioned muscles. When converting a pacer, changing direction also helps him understand that he has to trot while going in both directions, not just one.

After the horse trots consistently on the lunge line, his new gait can be further solidified under saddle. Posting to his trot will create an association that will help him remember his gait, as will a rider's encouragement and praise. But before you teach him to accept a rider, make note of these other physical considerations that apply to other driving-trained horses.

CONFORMATION CONCERNS

A horse bred specifically for a driving sport or pulling work may have conformation characteristics that aren't entirely suitable for riding. On the other hand, physical problems that make him a less-than-perfect driving horse may not be a problem at all in a riding horse.

A well-conformed driving horse shares most of the characteristics of the well-conformed riding horse: balance, proportion, correct legs, and hard, good-sized feet. But driving horses are more likely to have certain characteristics, including some obvious flaws. They may affect these horses under saddle.

SIZE

Standardbreds and driving-sport horses tend to be small to average in height and weight, since agility and speed are vital to their sports. In general, their size will prove adequate for most adult female and smaller male riders. Standardbreds in particular—who average just over 15 hands—may be too small for adult men to ride, even if their drivers were large men. A horse can pull at least twice the weight it can carry.

The opposite may be true if your prospect is a working draft horse. Strictly speaking, no horse is too large to be ridden. But some are too large to be easily fitted with ready-made saddles. You can find saddles with extra-wide trees, both English and Western, but these are really designed for horses with either prominent withers or broad Quarter

Horse–type shoulders, rather than horses with huge girth measurements.

But those too big to fit into an easily available saddle are rare. Doc and Prince are comfortable in regular Western saddles. Most draft horses probably will fit into Western saddles a little more easily than English, since they tend to have the low withers and broad shoulders of the stock-type breeds.

If you want to ride an extremely large draft horse, you may be faced with two options: spend a few thousand dollars on a custom-made saddle, or ride bareback. Look around first, though. Some warmbloods are nearly as big around the girth as draft horses, and there are plenty of ready-made saddles around that will fit them.

FEET

Both driving and riding horses require good feet to remain sound, but driving horses tend to have an extra advantage here. Most harness breeds have some cold blood, and one of the great benefits of that are big, hard feet.

But remember one fact before you assume that feet will be no problem for your retraining prospect—a hoof can be sound enough for driving but not sound enough for more than light riding. With weight on his back, a horse puts far more pounds-per-hoof pressure on his feet than does a horse being driven.

This is particularly true if the horse canters or gallops, something he rarely does under harness. At those gaits, there is a moment in each stride when all the weight of horse and rider is carried on one foot. An animal inclined to navicular disease, among other stress-related conditions, may show no problems under harness but can become lame under saddle.

A big horse destined to carry a light rider will probably remain as sound under saddle as he was under harness. But a light one, possibly a small Standardbred, intended for a large rider may have problems. Consult a farrier or a veterinarian for advice on trimming and pads that might help keep him sound.

PACING HORSE PECULIARITIES

Pacing horses sometimes have flaws that caused them no problems in their racing careers, but can lead to difficulties when they are switched to the trot and ridden. These include body length, body width, and leg correctness.

The pacing gait itself makes interference unlikely, but a horse might have conformation that would contribute to him brushing one foot against the other on the opposite corner at the trot. It's not that these conformation characteristics are desirable in pacers, but rather that their harmlessness hasn't stopped breeders from perpetuating them.

If your horse has any of them, they may cause your horse to have problems. They may, predictably, cause the horse to interfere or brush at the trot. They may also cause other complications as you retrain the horse.

The first characteristic is a short back. Many perfectly sound and successful pacers are remarkably short-backed. Since the pacer's legs on the same side move forward and back simultaneously at the racing gait, there has been no need to selectively breed horses with enough body length to prevent overreach. When ridden, this horse may interfere with himself at either a fast trot or a canter. A bigger problem may be finding a saddle and fittings that will stay in place. Arab tack sometimes works well for a pacer, since Arabs also have very short backs. But they have wider backs than pacers, so don't assume an Arab saddle will fit without trying it.

Pacers do tend to have fairly narrow bodies, again because there has been no need to breed for body width to prevent interference. Saddle pads usually take care of any problems of fit, unless the saddle tree is quite wide.

Finally, check your pacer for cow hocks, in which the hocks turn in while the rear toes turn out. This characteristic is highly undesirable in trotters and will have been actively selected against in breeding, but it causes fewer problems in pacers. Surprisingly, the feet of the cow-hocked horse often turn out only at the walk, but turn in at the trot. This also causes interference that doesn't occur at the pace.

There is no evidence that cow hocks actually help pacers go faster, but the characteristic is so prevalent, even among the stars of the sport, that some observers think it's an advantage. At the very least, it's not a problem.

For a horse that is expected to use at a fast trot, extreme cow hocks may be a problem. As stated in Chapter Three, cow hocks are common among Western performance horses, which are rarely asked for a fast trot. For a horse expected to be used at a walk, slow trot, or moderate canter, cow hocks should not be a problem.

HINDQUARTERS

The power in a pulling horse comes primarily from the front end rather than behind. That's directly opposite from galloping, jumping, and quick-turn sports. A driving horse that has powerful hindquarters and is relatively light in front will most likely make a better riding horse than he ever was a driving horse.

A horse well balanced for driving will probably be a little more front-heavy than what is ideal in a riding horse, but in most cases the variance won't be enough to make any difference in his usefulness. After all, the European warmblood breeds are, in general, equally good at driving and jumping.

Predictably, pacers tend to show the extreme in lightness of the hindquarters. Their gait requires little impulsion from the rear. Few pacers make good jumpers, but you may find an exception. Still, count on using a pacer for the flat rather than fences.

FOREQUARTERS

The value of weight in front for pulling causes breeders to select for necks a little heavier and shoulders a little deeper than you are likely to find in other horses of similar size. Withers can be either high and prominent or so low that they blend right into the back, and riders can have problems developing proper balance aboard driving-bred horses. Saddle fitting is sometimes difficult, even with a small driving horse, and you will probably find yourself experimenting with additional equipment.

Pacers tend to have high, fairly narrow withers and often need carefully adjusted padding as well as breastplates or breast collars to keep their saddles from slipping backward. Some trotting-bred driving horses need this kind of help too.

BACK

Horsemen, no matter what use they make of their animals, rarely like a horse with a long back. Long-backed horses, whether or not they have to carry weight on their backs, are more likely to become unsound.

The harness sports favor horses with short backs, since agility and maneuverability are important in all of the disciplines. Add this to the increased probability of soundness and the fact that you don't need space for a rider, and you'll find that harness breeds are often bred specifically for short backs.

This means that you'll find some driving horses with backs so short that you wonder if there's room for a saddle. There probably is, although it may have to be a small one and you will most likely have to use both a breastplate and a crupper. You'll also spend hours adjusting them.

Remember the converse, too. A driving horse with a back of normal or slightly greater-than-normal length may become available because he wasn't agile enough for his sport. He may be just fine for riding.

THE RETRAINING PROCESS

As in most retraining projects, converting a driving horse to riding requires less time than training an unbroken horse to ride. Most of the preliminary steps require minutes rather than days. In many cases, the first steps can be eliminated altogether. Go through them anyway, since they will help the horse get used to his new job gradually. Your first job will be to choose tack.

THE BRIDLE

A driving horse knows how to wear a bridle and how to respond to the bit. The average driving bridle is similar to an English bridle, usually featuring a snaffle bit. Most driving bits include a half cheek, a metal piece extending below the ring but not attached to the reins. Its effect is similar to that of a regular ringed snaffle, but the cheek helps to prevent the bit from pinching and pulling through.

Some driving horses are trained to use a liverpool bit with a straight mouth or a slight port. These act much like unjointed snaffles, except they feature rings to hook curb chains. If the chain has been fastened snugly, the horse will be familiar with the effects of a riding curb. In many cases, driving liverpools are used with loose curb chains, so the horses know how to respond to slightly leveraged snaffles.

Dave Bradham uses simple, ringed-snaffle driving bridles on his ridden draft horses, simply because they fit and the horses are comfortable with them. If you prefer, you may change to a riding snaffle, with either a jointed or straight mouthpiece.

Some driving horses have learned to use more elaborate bits, including driving curbs. Most will adjust well to a simple snaffle. Those who don't may require some bit experimentation.

Remember that many harness bridles are "closed." They include blinders or blinkers to restrict the horse's side vision. Although Bradham keeps blinders on Doc's and Prince's riding bridles, you may prefer an open bridle.

A horse who has never worn anything except a closed bridle should be led around for a few minutes while wearing his new bridle. He needs to get used to the idea of an unrestricted field of vision while at work.

Finally, harness horses—particularly race horses—often wear shadow rolls over their nosebands. Trainers believe these wide rolls of sheepskin or synthetic fabric keep horses from being distracted by shadows at their feet. Since racing harness also includes checkreins to keep horses' heads high, they usually manage well when allowed a natural head carriage with no shadow roll. They can take a look at anything that interests them.

Once the horse is comfortable in his bridle, you can test his response to the bit. Driving horses understand that a pull on a particular side of the bit requires their movement in that direction. But some, especially those used with sulkies and light carts, also expect to feel the rein on the side of the rump to which they are expected to turn or, sometimes, on the opposite side. They also may or may not respond to neck reining, depending upon the vehicle they pulled and the style of harness they used.

THE SADDLE

Unless your driving-trained horse is a huge draft animal, saddle fitting will not be a major problem. Since some driving breeds tend to have straight shoulders and fairly low withers, you will have to be careful about placing and fitting pads under some saddles. A horse with unusually low withers may need help keeping the saddle in place. Sometimes a crupper can be used to keep the saddle from slipping forward. An overgirth can also help.

A long girth or a tie strap is often necessary for a draft horse that is being retrained for riding.

A draft horse will usually need a wide tree saddle. He will also need a very long girth. The tie strap of the Western saddle ensures that the saddle can be attached to the widest-bodied horse.

The saddle itself and the process of being saddled and girthed will rarely upset a driving horse. Driving horses spend longer than riding horses being tacked up, handled, pushed, and maneuvered. They are used to extensive handling and adjusting of tack.

The weight and placement of the saddle are not likely to bother a horse who has done heavy work, since the harness saddle sits in the same place and is similar in weight to a light riding saddle. A horse who has worked in a lighter harness may notice the difference in saddle weight, but this won't make him object.

Both light and heavy driving horses will have worn a fairly snug girth, and you should have no trouble securing the saddle. But you should be careful not to tighten the girth suddenly. Harness girths are worn a bit looser than most riding girths, and a driving horse will not have developed the nasty habit of puffing out his belly to prevent tightening of the girth. You don't want him to develop that vice at this stage of his working life.

Dave Bradham likes to let the horse see and smell both the pad and the saddle before placing them on his back. A good look and sniff help prevent the horse from believing that a predator has suddenly landed on his back.

The stirrups will be unfamiliar to a driving horse. Try leading the horse around with stirrups dangling. He probably won't react at all, since harness horses carry so many straps and so much other equipment that movement and pressure rarely frighten them. If he does react, you need to do a little work on the problem. If his concern is minor, lead him around enough times so that he loses his concern. If the problem is more severe, you may choose to go to the lunge line. Work first with stirrups tied as the horse is lunged, then with stirrups loose.

MOUNTING

Some driving horses are ridden as part of their work, so yours may accept mounting immediately. Others, like Prince and Doc, were never

The horse should be allowed to see and sniff new equipment.

ridden before but are so good-natured that they don't object. Others object strenuously. Usually, the objections are minor and easily over-come.

Some trainers like to try the first mounting with the horse in his regular driving harness. There's tradition behind this. In the past, when horses did heavy labor, farmers and other drivers would often leave heavy equipment in the field and return the horse to the barn by hop-ping aboard and riding home. For a horse that is being retrained, this procedure has the advantage of the horse learning the first step of his new career in his familiar tack.

Dave Bradham does this, finding that well-trained draft horses readily accept it. But unless you are very secure and confident in your horse's probable response to the presence of a rider, you should approach the first mounting as if he were an unbroken horse. Do this in an enclosed area, and ask a friend to help. You'll need someone to hold the bridled horse through each step; although the hold can be increas-ingly lighter as the horse demonstrates his willingness to cooperate.

First, standing on a mounting block or bale of hay, lay a little of your weight on the horse's saddled back. He will probably accept this, but he may become nervous after a few seconds. It's not the weight that may alarm the horse, but rather the presence of something that moves, however slightly. Step away just as the horse indicates that he's becoming nervous by trying to step away himself. Don't stay so long that he becomes frightened. Wait just until the slightly restive point. Try this a few times, holding your weight against him longer each time. When he can tolerate this for several minutes, partially mount with one foot in the stirrup. Don't insert your foot beyond the front of the instep. You don't want to be dragged if he raises a sudden, strenuous objection. After he accepts this for a minute or so, get aboard and sit quietly as long as the horse remains calm. Talk to him soothingly, taking advantage of the harness horse's training to verbal cues. Use the word "Whoa"

The first ride should be short and undemanding.

when he starts to move. When more than minor restiveness appears, get off. Extend the time you stay aboard with each repeat.

THE AIDS

Once the horse stands consistently with a rider, ask him to move forward. Most harness horses are sound-oriented and will respond to a click of the tongue or verbal commands such as "Move on" and "Walk on." Experiment to see which words help your horse move out. Dave Bradham found that verbal commands worked with Prince and Doc.

"When I hopped on them, they didn't know what to do," he says. "They just stood there. It was the regular voice commands that I used while driving them that worked."

Harness horses sometimes respond to a jiggle of the reins, but you probably don't want your riding horse to need this kind of aid

Harness-trained horses will not
understand leg aids at first.

A direct rein in combination with the leg aids will soon teach him that both mean to turn.

indefinitely. Use it, if necessary, but combine it with other cues and phase out rein movement as quickly as possible.

After you have discovered which cue the horse responds to, use it along with gentle leg pressure on or just behind the girth. Harness-trained horses don't understand leg aids, so you must make sure to combine them with signals that they do understand.

The process of teaching leg aids shouldn't take long, since the basic cues make sense to the horse mentality. Horses try to escape pressure, and leg aids take advantage of this. The cue to move on, pressure of both legs on the sides, encourages the horse to escape by moving forward.

Harness-trained horses do understand the normal direct-rein signals to turn, and these should be used as you work on turns and changes of direction. Use the normal riding-horse aid for turns, which is pressure just behind the girth on the opposite side from the turn. This pressure will encourage a horse to move away from it. That's the direction you are looking for. Even if the horse doesn't quite grasp the concept, use of the correct leg aid in addition to the direct-rein signal will teach him that the two mean the same thing.

THE CANTER

Most harness-trained horses will have never been asked for a canter. They may have done it, but every time they cantered they would have been pulled back to a trot or pace and probably criticized.

A harness horse at the trot or pace interprets the request for greater speed as a faster trot or pace, not a canter. You may have to work hard to convince him that it's finally acceptable for him to run. Begin with straight-line cantering.

Strictly speaking, since the horse has an almost insurmountable inclination to bend slightly in the direction of his leading leg, no horse canters in a straight line. But for the purposes of his initial training at the canter, ask only for the gait for a few strides in the center line of the ring or along the straight line of the rail.

Don't worry about leads at this point. Your harness-trained horse won't have a clue about your request for a particular lead, and you can't teach him until he canters consistently in a straight line at your request. Some trainers prefer to teach the canter on a bend, relying on the horse's natural instinct to take the correct lead on a turn. But a big, heavy horse who takes the incorrect lead on a turn can be dangerously unbalanced, particularly if he is not used to the gait. A Standardbred will probably do it fine, but for safety's sake, begin on the straight.

At a steady trot, urge the horse into greater speed with a lessening of rein pressure, a cluck, or a verbal command to canter, plus pressure on both sides just slightly behind the girth. If he merely trots faster, slow him by taking back slightly and lessening the leg aids. Then try again.

It may take a number of tries, but the horse should eventually canter. Praise him when he does, and repeat the process until you can produce several strides of canter consistently.

Once the horse has learned to do a willing canter in reasonable balance at your request, you may begin to teach him how to take the correct lead. Choose a corner or other obvious bend to ask for the canter. This serves two purposes: First, it takes advantage of his natural inclination to choose the correct lead for a turn. Second, it allows you to give an aid that will help his hindquarters select the leg positioning which will force the correct leading leg in front.

Urge the horse into the canter as you have been doing, but bring the outside leg—the opposite one from the turn—a little further behind the girth and squeeze. This pressure prompts the horse to take off in the canter with that hind leg, forcing the correct foreleg to lead the gait.

Practice the canter both around turns and on the straightaway. The harness-trained horse may not be used to bending well around turns, and you will have to be careful to keep his head, neck, and hindquarters moving in the correct arc.

STOPPING AND BACKING

Harness horses get plenty of work backing up, and they understand the concept well. They will understand only some of the rider's cues, but they may understand others better than the average riding horse. Your harness-trained horse will slow when he feels rein pressure and will stop if the pressure becomes great enough. He will stop better if he hears a verbal cue. That can be "Stop" or "Halt," but it's most likely to be "Whoa."

Some harness horses are trained to the voice as their primary cue. Dave Bradham's pair know to stop instantly when they hear "Whoa."

"In fact," he says, "they'll stop if somebody in the crowd says it." If your horse understands English that well, you can use the ability as you develop the other, more traditional, stopping cues for the ridden horse. You may continue using these voice cues as you ride the horse, but if you'd rather not, use them in conjunction with rein cues until the horse responds to either.

The horse will not understand the purpose of the leg squeeze prior to the stop. You may apply it, very gently, so as not to confuse him, and he will begin to collect himself at the stop even though he doesn't know what he's doing. The squeeze urges his hindquarters under him while he comes to a halt.

He will also not understand the leg squeeze that commands him to back, but he will understand give-and-take rein pressure, along with the word "Back." Again combine what he knows with the additional aid you want to use until he responds to any combination of the backing cues.

The process of mounting and training for cues has been very much like that followed in training a young horse. The difference between training an unbroken horse and retraining a driving horse will be that instead of each step requiring a day or more, the entire process may be accomplished in one day, two at the most.

In fact, you may find it moving so quickly that you're tempted to skip steps. Resist the temptation. The horse needs a chance to absorb the requirements of his new work in a sensible order, and you need a chance to identify problem areas if they develop.

CHAPTER SEVEN

Riding to Driving

EVEN THOUGH DRIVING CAN BE MUCH more expensive than riding, pleasure driving is among the fastest growing equestrian sports. Not only is cost an issue, but it's also far more difficult to find a place to do it. Nevertheless, people by the thousands are turning from riding to driving, and there are several very good reasons for it.

An aging population of riders has contributed a big pool of people looking for safer and less strenuous equestrian activities. With a well-trained horse and equipment in good condition, driving is safer than riding.

If you do have a taste for danger, you can find driving sports to suit you. There are obstacle competitions, cross-country events, and even ice racing. Or you can try driving on a highway. But for most of us, driving presents much less risk of falling, pulling muscles, or having our backs jarred.

For people concerned with agility rather than injury, it is easier to keep doing well in driving than in riding in spite of advancing age. In the past few years, there have been open national driving champions eligible to collect Social Security checks. The same is not true of riding competitions.

Most kinds of driving are also easier on horses, a fact not lost on owners of older or slightly unsound horses. The absence of a rider's weight leads to less stress on a horse's legs, feet, and back. There is weight involved, of course, but its effect is dramatically lessened by wheels or sleigh runners. The drag that remains is absorbed through the horse's chest, shoulders, and barrel.

This is not to say that legs aren't important to a driving horse; they are, and a hopelessly unsound riding horse isn't going to become miraculously sound once a harness is fastened to him. But forelegs, the most common site of unsoundness in a riding horse, are less stressed in a driving horse.

Hind legs are more important, since the hindquarters provide much of the impulsion that allows forward movement in the driving horse. But the power comes mostly from the area above the hocks, so minor unsoundness or conformation flaws below that point rarely affect a horse's ability to pull. Even poor hock conformation rarely leads to the unsoundness in a driving horse that it would in a riding horse, possibly because the walk and a modest trot are the most common driving gaits.

Driving is certainly easier on an outgrown horse or pony, as we discussed in Chapters One and Two. If you want to keep and use the pony but everybody in the family is too big to ride him, you'll have to teach him to drive.

Other people turn to driving as an off-season activity. You can drive your horse in a sleigh rather than keep him in the barn. In more temperate climates, winter may be the off-season anyway. A horse often needs a physical or mental break from his regular sport. Driving may be a low-stress alternative that provides variety for both horse and rider.

Driving can provide off-season sport, too. Hundreds of Quarter Horses are retrained to drive in cutter and chariot racing during the winter, primarily in the mountain states of Utah, Wyoming, and Idaho. In this sport, horses race as pairs, pulling special, lightweight carts at the gallop. Most of the horses involved are racing Quarter Horses, and some of them return to regular racing in the spring. Others are a little too old to be successful under saddle but are more competitive under harness. It's an odd sport, but an exciting one, and it proves that a breed known more for its slow walk and fast gallop can work well in harness.

In some breeds, driving is a well-established part of breed competition. Saddlebreds, Arabs, and Morgans are often switched between riding and driving. But other breed organizations have recently begun featuring driving competitions, too. Twenty years ago, you wouldn't have seen Quarter Horses under harness in sanctioned events. Today, driving classes are scheduled in most large breed shows.

All of these situations have two things in common: Almost all of the horses involved were ridden first. And almost all of the people involved were riders first.

SUITABILITY FOR DRIVING

Strictly speaking, any horse capable of being ridden is capable of being driven. But some are better candidates for success.

Size is usually not a consideration in picking likely candidates for casual driving. Harnesses and vehicles are available for every size pony or horse. Since a horse can pull several times more weight than he can carry, every horse or pony can pull at least one adult in a cart or sleigh.

Size only becomes a consideration when you have a specific vehicle or a specific kind of driving in mind for a particular horse. On a smooth, level surface at a walk or slow trot, a horse of normal size can pull nearly its own weight in vehicle and passengers. Many horses can pull more.

A light-boned horse, a horse being asked to travel a route with hills, or one being driven over a rough road will be able to manage less weight. Any demand for speed also limits the weight that a horse can pull.

Estimate the size of the vehicle you hope to use, add the weights of the passengers that you hope it will carry, and choose your retraining prospect accordingly. If you don't have a vehicle, choose your horse or pony first and look for the cart or carriage later. You can begin retraining well before you actually have the vehicle.

Don't forget that the size of the shafts count, too. Some horses are too wide or too narrow for particular shafts. Shafts can be changed, but it's not cheap and it's not always easy to find a carriage maker to do it.

There's one other point to consider in relation to size. Bigger is often not better when the driving activity requires agility. Horses used in driving trials, where obstacle courses are traveled and speed counts, are rarely much larger than 15 hands. What a bigger horse gains in pulling power, he loses in the ability to negotiate turns and tight spots.

The psychological characteristics of a horse are probably more important than physical traits in picking a likely horse for driving. The best driving horses are calm, slow to react to unexpected sights and sounds, and willing to stand quietly for long periods of time. Nervous, jumpy horses can be trained to drive, but it will take a long time and a great deal of work to make them trustworthy.

The only horse mentally unsuitable for driving is the one that dislikes anything behind him. Don't waste ten minutes trying to retrain a kicker, no matter how good he is in every other way. Think long and hard about trying to teach driving to a horse that jumps or pins his ears when anyone moves behind him. It can probably be done, but neither he nor you will enjoy it.

Dave Bradham, who has trained horses of different breeds and backgrounds for use in his carriage business, says attitude is the primary factor in his decision to begin training.

"You have to see how they act with something behind them," he says. "It's the most important thing."

While someone holds the horse, walk behind him—out of kicking range, of course—and talk, move, and gesture. The horse doesn't have to be oblivious, but if he's more than curious or slightly suspicious, be suspicious yourself. A frightened or angry horse may never settle down enough to be driven safely and successfully.

A horse that can't stand car traffic can be driven, and you may enjoy teaching him and using him provided you have a space to drive far away from motor vehicles. That's impossible for most people, so make a traffic-shy horse your last choice for retraining to drive.

Physical characteristics are less limiting. Only incurable unsoundness will make a horse totally unsuitable. Minor unsoundness can often be tolerated in a horse that is required only to walk or trot for limited periods on a suitable surface.

Foot and pastern problems can be a factor if you expect to drive the horse on pavement for extended periods. Soreness may not show up on grass or dirt, but the concussion contributed by hard surfaces may make the horse unsuitable for your intended use. Consult a veterinarian or farrier for advice on training, pads, or special shoeing.

HARNESS

There are two basic kinds of harness. One features a breast collar and is designed for light use. The other utilizes a neck collar and is intended for heavy pulling. The breast-collar harness is less complicated, lighter in weight, and more similar to riding tack. Moreover, it's far easier than neck-collar harness to fit correctly.

Fit is an important consideration for a member of a breed not tra-ditionally used for driving, perhaps one with narrow or sloping shoul-ders or high withers. Because fitting is easy, breast-collar harness is the best choice for training any horse being converted to harness. It may be

*This team of Suffolks is wearing
neck-collar harness for heavy pulling.*

This pacer is in breast-collar harness for lighter work.

the permanent choice for a horse that is intended to pull a light cart or sleigh. Breast-collar harness also shows off good conformation, making it the only choice for most breed competition.

Safe harness that won't break under stress is important with any horse in any driving activity, but it's especially important with an adult horse being converted from riding. These horses have certainly been asked to canter or gallop during their previous careers, and they won't be reluctant to do it if a broken strap whacks them on the hindquarters while setting them free.

Check a used harness for rotting or brittleness, particularly under and around buckles and hooks. Look underneath the straps as well as on top, since rotting begins on the unfinished side.

Ideally, you will begin training a new horse in a new harness. If your finances don't run to new leather, consider nylon harness. It's cheaper, wears better, washes well, and is usually lighter than leather harness. It's a good choice for training, even if you feel you must move on to leather later for competition or appearance.

For safe driving in general and training in particular, properly fitted harness is a must. "Whatever harness you're using, make sure it fits the horse," Dave Bradham says. "'Almost' isn't good enough."

Badly fitted harness is dangerous to horse and driver. Retrained horses are no more vulnerable to the dangers of poor fit than young horses, but they may be a little more difficult to fit, tempting the trainer to make do with something that's not quite right.

Harness makers produce a limited range of sizes, relying on the fact that almost every strap is adjustable. Occasionally, the straps can't be adjusted enough to fit a particular horse.

The withers of a warmblood, for example, might pull the breast collar too high on the chest, no matter how much you let down the neckpiece strap that holds it in place. Breeching, the rear-end equivalent of the breast collar, may not fit a horse with particularly wide or narrow

Fitting a pony to harness can be particularly challenging.

hindquarters. Individual sections of harness can be replaced, and you may have to experiment to get the proper fit.

Ponies can be particularly hard to fit. Complete harness is usually available in only one pony size, so if your pony is extremely large or small you may have to do considerable interchanging of harness parts. A 10-hand Shetland may need a pony harness with extra holes to make it smaller, while a 14-hand Welsh may need a harness with extra holes to make it larger.

Proper fit also matters when you choose a bit. Fit, in this case, means suitability to the horse's personality as well as the actual size of his mouth.

In most cases, a horse changing from riding to driving should be trained in a simple jointed snaffle. You can use a straight-mouth snaffle if the horse has been ridden in one and is particularly sensitive to the bit.

There is no reason that you can't buckle a riding snaffle onto his driving bridle, but most driving horses are trained and driven with the driving equivalent. The driving snaffle usually features cheek pieces, with the full cheek, including pieces that extend above and below the rings. The half cheek, the most common driving bit nowadays, has the cheek piece only below the ring. Since the cheek pieces are not attached to curb straps, their action is essentially the same as a ringed riding snaffle, with a couple of exceptions.

The cheek pieces serve to prevent the bit from pulling through the mouth, a circumstance slightly more likely to occur in driving, since rein signals have to be a little stronger in the absence of leg aids. But they also keep the bit a little more stationary in the mouth, and this can make it more severe than a riding snaffle. Your riding-to-driving horse may not respond well to the lack of give in the bit.

A riding horse that has been used with a D-ring or eggbutt snaffle will find the effects of the driving snaffle similar and may be comfortable with an immediate change to a driving bit. One that has been ridden only with a loose-ringed snaffle may need a more gradual change.

A horse that needed a curb bit while being ridden may need the driving equivalent, the liverpool. The effect is similar, although the liverpool usually permits different chain-attachment points. This allows the bit to be altered from a snaffle-like effect to a severe curb.

VEHICLE

Although you will be following several steps and using other equipment before you harness the horse to a vehicle, you may begin looking for and making decisions about the horse's first cart well before he's actually ready to be hitched. If you have trained before, you may already have one. Otherwise, you will need to buy or borrow a suitable training cart. For safety's sake, it should be sturdy and easy to exit quickly. Most horses are hitched for the first time to a light, wide-based, two-wheeled cart. This makes sense for retraining adult horses as well as young, green ones.

You may be tempted, particularly with a previously trained, well-behaved adult horse, to skip the two-wheeled, easy-access cart and hitch directly to a more elaborate vehicle. It's been done, but some trainers have found it disastrous for both themselves and the vehicle.

GROUND TRAINING

You may know the training background of your horse. A well-trained riding horse was almost certainly lunged prior to being ridden, and an extremely well-trained one may have been driven in long reins. One trained by a meticulous old-timer may have even learned to pull a training cart in a manner nearly identical to a driving-trained horse.

Any of these early lessons will give your horse a head start in learning his new job. A horse broken by someone whose training philosophy consisted of climbing aboard and trying to stay on will require a little more work. But even he should be easier to train than a green horse.

LUNGEING

Time-saving begins immediately. Lungeing is a vital first step in training an unbroken young horse to drive. It's usually begun in the same way as with a riding horse—that is, with the line attached to a bitless cavesson or plain halter. The young horse learns control and balance before his mouth is ready for a bit. Gradually the bridle and bit are added, either over or under the cavesson but not attached to the lunge line. Sometimes other harness parts are added too, but the presence of the bit in the mouth is most important. By the time the young driving horse is ready to progress to long reining, he's used to the bit.

The previously trained horse will be used to the bit and will not need the gradual introduction during lungeing. He may not need to have his gaits developed or to learn balance and control either. You can probably move directly to long reining with most trained adult horses, but you would be well-advised to go through a session or two of lungeing anyway.

Lungeing provides a natural progression to long reining, which you must do before hitching the horse to a vehicle, no matter how well he behaves while being handled or ridden. It prepares the horse for the physical and psychological control he will experience under harness.

There are other aspects of retraining that you can begin during lungeing. You may use the sessions to begin training the horse to respond to voice cues, which are more important in driving than in riding. During the training periods give verbal cues to start and stop, using the lungeing whip for emphasis.

You may also, while the horse wears only a halter, begin to get him accustomed to being touched in ways and in places he's unused to from his previous training. Dave Bradham does this very early in the process of training to drive.

"Take a pole and start touching their bellies and legs," he says. "You want to see how they act and get them used to it."

Some trainers will use a gentle touch of the lungeing whip to do this, but others believe that using a whip rather than a pole makes the touching seem like punishment. The pressure and touching should be perceived as a fact of life that the horse has to accept, not punishment for some misdeed.

LONG REINING

Although it is called *ground driving* by driving trainers and *long reining* in training for riding, the two terms basically mean the same thing. The bridled horse, with two long reins attached to the bit, is directed around an enclosure, learning to respond to the requests to go faster, slow down, turn, stop, and back. It is possible to train a riding horse without long reining, but it's invariably used in training for driving. Long reining is the vital last step before introducing and hitching a horse or pony to a vehicle.

If your riding horse was long reined when young, you and he are fortunate because he'll already know most of what he needs to about driving. He'll only need a little time on the long reins before being introduced to the vehicle. Even if he was moved directly to a saddle from lungeing, he won't need nearly as much work on the long lines as

*Long reining is an important final step before
hitching the pony or horse to his vehicle.*

the young driving horse, since he already understands directions given through the bit.

Riding and driving trainers tend to long rein slightly differently, and the procedure used by driving trainers is obviously more conducive to driving. A riding horse that was given solid basic training can be taken through the driving-horse procedure or, if you feel he will be more comfortable, can be reintroduced to long reining with the riding-horse procedure. You may discover, however, that he was long reined in the same way as a driving horse. The two methods are sometimes used interchangeably by riding trainers.

The most common long-reining procedure for training riding horses is to attach the bit rings to reins after the horse has accepted the bridle and bit while still lungeing with a cavesson or halter. These reins may be either draw reins or side reins attached to a surcingle around his belly, or long reins held in two hands by the trainer. Eventually, all horses are controlled through long reins attached to the bit. The surcingle is usually left on to maintain the association between girth pressure and rein control, even if the surcingle is not attached to reins of any kind.

Some driving trainers do use the surcingle and side-rein procedure, but the driving horse is more likely to be introduced to a bitting harness, light harness, or collar harness before the long reins are used. The minimum for ground driving is usually a surcingle, harness saddle, and crupper. The horse is permitted to get used to harness in the stall or ring, or lunged with harness under a halter or cavesson. After he accepts the harness as nonthreatening and comfortable, he will be led, allowed to wander in a paddock, or asked to stand.

Only after he's used to harness does ground driving in long reins begin, with a helper available to control the head and the trainer walking behind, out of kicking range, using the reins to teach turns and stops. The instruction is reinforced by the helper.

The previously trained horse is going to need very little work on learning rein signals to turn and stop, having already learned them with a rider on his back. He will have to get used to the feel of harness and the presence of a trainer behind him. So driving-style long reining is important for the riding-trained horse, although the emphasis will be different. You'll spend more time helping him get used to the harness and less time on the signals to turn.

Even if you prefer to begin long reining with partial harness, you should accustom the horse to full harness before you complete this phase of training. First to go on is the driving bridle. Some trainers like to use a closed bridle—one with blinders—as part of the long-reining harness, while others prefer an open bridle during this step, moving to a closed bridle only when the cart is ready to be attached.

The open bridle permits the horse to see the trainer and check out some of what goes on behind him, giving him confidence and satisfaction. Many riding horses, used to being able to see much of the area towards their hindquarters, are happier in open bridles during both retraining and driving; others are confident in their trainers and are better off not seeing behind them. There's no hard-and-fast rule for a retrained horse. You will have to make the decision based on the horse's personality and his reaction to each step.

Bridle fitting is sometimes a problem for riding-bred horses, that tend to have smaller heads than driving-bred horses like draft breeds and many Standardbreds. If your harness was made for these breeds, you may have to make sure that the various straps are carefully adjusted to fit snugly but not too tightly.

Ponies can be a challenge in bridle fitting. Some of them have big heads, very small ears, and bristly manes and forelocks that push the headpiece too high to remain behind the ears. You may have to clip a bridle path, including the forelock area, to make sure that the bridle doesn't pull off over the ears.

The riding-trained horse should not object to most parts of the harness. The bridle, breast collar, harness saddle, and girth should go on with no resistance. The breeching will be less familiar, although a horse whose turnout blanket included leg straps probably won't object to a strap being fastened around his hindquarters.

The crupper annoys most horses, and a riding-trained one will be no exception. In fact, he will probably object even more energetically to a strap being buckled right under his tail for the first time in his life.

*Most horses don't like the crupper, so
its fitting has to be done with care.*

There are precautions you can take to make the procedure as pleasant as possible. First, try to fit the backstrap that runs from the harness saddle to the crupper before you put the crupper in place. This strap is adjustable, but don't assume that a middle hole will be appropriate. Lay the strap on the horse's back and estimate where the crupper will have to be fastened. Guess long rather than short. If you have to make adjustments once the crupper is in place, you don't want to be trying desperately to loosen the crupper on a kicking, bucking horse.

After the backstrap and crupper are adjusted for size, place the crupper carefully under the tail, making sure that no hairs are caught. The crupper should fit up against the root of the tail, but not so tightly that it pinches the sensitive skin.

A horse that reacts badly to the introduction of the crupper can be accustomed to it more gradually, even with breakable twine taking the place of the backstrap while the horse stands with the crupper in place. Some trainers object to this idea, believing that you don't want a horse to realize that he can break a backstrap to give himself relief, but others find that it works.

Work in the crupper should be short at first, with the time extended each day. The skin under the tail is sensitive and requires time to toughen.

Attach the long reins to the bit, run them through the saddle terrets, and take one rein in each hand. You may be able to do the basic long-rein work alone if your horse was long reined as a young riding horse, but you should call on a helper if you have doubts. Someone at the horse's head will help speed the process of reinforcing signals and learning new ones. You may leave a halter on, over or under the harness bridle, so the header has something to handle. You may attach a short lead rope for further control.

A previously broken horse may require neither halter nor lead. The header can grasp the bridle if emergency help is required, but he shouldn't touch the horse if he doesn't have to.

Driving trainers usually begin long reining while standing further back than riding trainers do, but the first lessons are usually conducted with the trainer slightly to the inside rather than directly behind. As the horse accepts the presence of the person behind him, the trainer moves further and further back until he's directly behind the horse.

Use a voice command to try to move the horse out. The actual command doesn't matter, but it should be the word or phrase you plan to use while driving. It may be "Walk on," "Walk," "Forward," or "Get up." If the horse doesn't respond, you have several options for reinforcement. A header can step forward to encourage the movement, pulling on a lead rope if necessary. If you don't have a header, you may jiggle the reins or touch the horse very lightly with a whip. Whichever reinforcement you choose, make sure to use the voice command first. You don't want the horse to learn to respond to the reinforcement rather than the voice command.

Move forward at the walk until the horse is completely comfortable and moving steadily in his harness. Using the perimeter of a ring will allow you to keep moving without having to add turn signals, since the horse will probably make his own turns.

A horse that doesn't follow the outline of the ring may have to be encouraged to do so with slight direct-rein pull. After the horse has been around the ring a few times at the walk, you can begin turning to the center. Most riding-trained horses will turn immediately on the direct rein and will need only to practice doing it without the help of leg aids.

The rare riding horse that has only been neck reined will require reinforcement for his turns. If you are working with a header, have him direct the horse in his turns as you apply the direct rein. If you're working alone, you can try a very light tap with the whip on the side opposite from the direction of the turn.

Some riding-trained horses turn too abruptly. A sharp turn is fine for a horse that has only his body to worry about, but it's unsuitable for a horse that is pulling a vehicle. Work with the horse on controlled turns by adding an indirect rein to keep the turn wide and sweeping, rather than short and abrupt. Western-trained horses sometimes turn too much on a very light rein signal, especially those that learned a spin or rollback.

Long reining should be done at all gaits, even though the canter is rarely used in driving. You want the horse to get used to the feel of the harness at each gait while he's still in a safe, training situation. A horse that accidentally breaks into a canter while pulling a vehicle may discover that the crupper pulls and pinches. He may run faster, kick the vehicle, or bolt out of control. So let him feel what it's like to canter in a situation that you can control.

There's an added benefit to working on the canter on the long reins. You want the horse to learn how to be brought back to a trot or walk from a canter with voice cues or rein cues.

Prompt the faster gaits the same way you prompt moving out, with a voice cue plus any necessary reinforcement. The faster the gait, the longer the reins will have to be. You will also need to be nearer to the center of the ring to keep up. Because long reining at the faster gaits loses much of its resemblance to driving, you will be doing most of your retraining work following behind at the walk.

Riding horses have learned to slow in response to a pull on the reins, and you will use this signal as you retrain. You will also, simultaneously, use the appropriate vocal cue. If slowing within the same gait, you say "Slow," or whatever other word you choose as you apply the reins. When slowing to the next slower gait say "Trot," or "Walk." If you want the horse to stop altogether you can say "Stop," or "Halt." But most horses naturally respond to "Whoa."

After the horse has learned to be controlled through long reins, he has to learn something that he never experienced as a riding horse—the feel of weight pulling back on his chest or neck. There are several methods for introducing the horse to this experience.

Dave Bradham uses poles. "Attach poles directly to the saddle and lead the horse around," he suggests. "He drags the poles behind him and gets used to the pull."

Other trainers will fit a rope around the horse's chest and have a helper stand behind the horse holding the ends of the rope. The helper and trainer both have to be out of kicking range. As the horse is urged forward, the helper pulls on the ends of the rope, creating resistance. It's an instantly adjustable method of getting the horse used to the chest pressure. You can make the pull feel heavy or light, and you can get out of the way quickly if problems develop.

Next come the shafts, something else that a riding horse has never experienced. If your vehicle has permanently fastened shafts, try to find some old shafts that don't belong to any vehicle, or make a U-shaped set with light, inexpensive PVC pipes and plumbers' right-angle joints.

This step teaches the horse to be comfortable with shafts, showing him that they are not horse traps or any other terrible thing his imagination might suggest. Some trainers leave the shafts stationary and move the horse. Others move the shafts and keep the horse standing still.

Dave Bradham walks the horse around the shafts, giving him a good look. "Then I have somebody hold the shafts," he says. "I back the horse up and have the shafts put down." Eventually, the horse learns to be calm as the shafts are moved around him. He's also calm being moved near the shafts.

For some horses, the next step is to learn to pull a drag. This is a weight that bridges the gap between a driver on foot and one in a vehicle. The drag may consist of shafts or ropes attached to a tire or a block of wood, fastened to the harness saddle. The horse is long reined with the pull between himself and the walking trainer. He learns to accept the weight, the noise, and the inflexibility of something behind him. If he finds it upsetting and begins to kick, he's less likely to injure himself or his driver than if he were attached to a cart without this intermediate step. He also won't destroy an expensive piece of equipment.

Other trainers find the drag unnecessary. "Once you get to that point," Dave Bradham says, "you pretty well know what the horse is going to do around a cart."

Your horse's acceptance of the previous steps will tell you if you need the precaution of a drag. A calm horse that hasn't been alarmed or annoyed by any of the previous steps can be introduced directly to a cart.

But you still have to be careful, even with a horse that you think will accept the cart. "Have somebody head him," Bradham says. "And make sure you're in an enclosed area."

THE FIRST DRIVE

Before you hitch the horse or pony, let him have a very good look at the vehicle and make sure that he knows what it's going to sound like. His first encounter with it should be entirely visual.

It's safest to introduce the horse to the vehicle, not the other way around. The procedure should be repeated with any new vehicle, no matter how well the horse is trained.

"Even with a trained horse, I walk him up to it," Dave Bradham says. "I show it to him before I do anything else with it."

The horse can be haltered or under harness. Lead him to the cart, permit him to nuzzle it if he wishes, and lead him around it. After he

Let the pony have a good look at his first vehicle while it's still stationary.

Let the horse hear the vehicle in motion before he's hitched to it.

has made a thorough investigation, ask a helper to pick up the shafts and pull the cart away. Have it pulled in front of the horse, alongside him, and behind him. He should be able to hear the noise it makes while he's watching and while he can't see it.

Next, the horse must see and hear the cart move as he moves himself. You may do this with only a halter, but the horse will learn more if you harness him for long reining first. Listening to the movement of the cart while he's under harness provides a good simulation of the actual driving experience.

Before the cart is brought up behind the horse, there is one additional step that should be taken. He must learn to accept the pressure across his hindquarters that comes when he stops in a heavy vehicle or goes downhill in even a light one. He will have had no similar experience as a saddle horse.

"They absolutely have to be able to take the pressure across the back end," Bradham says. He likes to check them early for their reaction. "I'll have somebody on either side with a rope. They put pressure with the rope and you can see how the horse responds." The trainer remains at the head, restraining the horse with a lead rope and with voice signals.

Most horses are inclined to move forward when they are pushed from behind, so the driving horse has to learn that weight across the hindquarters is not a cue. Some horses despise the pressure and never learn to tolerate it, but most can be taught to allow their rear ends to act as a brake.

Some trainers are ready to hitch the horse to the cart as soon as he has accepted the sight and sound of its movement behind him. If your horse has shown no fear or restiveness during the process of harness fitting, long reining, and listening to the cart, you may go ahead and hitch. But you may feel more secure with an additional step.

With one person at the horse's head, the other lifts the shafts and pushes them into place on either side of the horse's body, making sure that the cart doesn't bump the hindquarters. They aren't attached, and when the horse is led or driven forward, the cart is pushed to keep up with him. If the horse kicks or struggles, he can be led out of the shafts and away from danger to himself or the vehicle.

This is exhausting work, and you probably won't be able to keep it up for more than a few minutes. But it will give the horse an excellent preview of what it will sound and feel like to have a cart traveling directly behind him.

Very cautious trainers sometimes pull shoes for the first few times a horse is hitched to a vehicle. This precaution has a double purpose. It makes any unexpected kick less destructive to people and vehicles, and it also makes the horse concentrate on where he's putting his feet rather than the frightening thing that's happening behind him.

If you have the horse's shoes removed, keep a close watch on his feet. Training trips on pavement need to be short and slow with an unshod horse. Excessive wear leads to sore feet, which give the horse an unpleasant introduction to his new career.

Initial hitching is done most safely with three people, one on either side of the horse and the third bringing up the shafts and cart behind. The two handlers can fully control the head as well as simultaneously insert the shafts into the tugs as the cart comes up behind. The traces can then be quickly fastened.

A calm horse can be hitched by two or even one person, but first hitching can cause unexpected fear and rebellion. A horse is most easily controlled in an emergency if he can be held on both sides and he's either completely hitched or completely free, not half attached and half not.

After the cart is secured, the horse should be led around for as long as necessary to calm him and make sure he stays that way. The safest procedure is to lead him with one person on either side of his head, each holding a rein. With a horse that appears calm enough, you can thread the reins through the terrets on the harness saddle and take your long-reining place alongside or behind the cart.

The helper should remain at the head, leading the horse for the first few circuits then walking beside his head as the driver takes over control. The helper should gradually move farther away to ensure that the horse is responding to the voice, rein cues, and whip of the driver, and not simply following the helper.

How long you need to remain on the ground depends upon the horse. One that has moved quickly and happily through each of the training steps without fighting the process and now, at this stage, remains calm, may be ready almost immediately to be driven from the cart. A tense horse may need several ground-driving lessons while pulling the cart.

Long reining should have taught the horse to slow and stop on rein and voice signals, and you can start working on these skills as soon as he is fully calm while pulling the cart. Remember that he will feel pressure from his breeching strap as the shafts absorb the weight of the vehicle. This may surprise or annoy a horse that's always been able to stop with no extraneous pieces of equipment pushing into him. Be ready to use your voice and hands to steady him.

The former riding horse is developed as a driving horse in the same way a young horse is—by regular, short lessons in which he's asked to do a lot of things that he can do easily and a few that are more difficult.

No matter how many different experiences he had as a saddle horse, he should, at least initially, be treated as a green horse. He has to be introduced to other horses pulling vehicles, to automobile traffic, and to surfaces that might cause his harness or cart to jiggle and pull. Even if he happily walked along the rutted shoulder of a road carrying a rider, he may now look at cars and ruts differently, knowing that he's less mobile and flexible while pulling a cart.

PART FOUR

Teaching New Sports

CHAPTER EIGHT

Dressage

A T ITS HIGHEST LEVELS, DRESSAGE IS the most sophisticated and elegant event in international equestrian competition. But at its most basic, dressage is nothing more than a systematic program of training that helps a horse reach his physical and mental potential. Even the United States Dressage Federation, which organizes this training program into a competitive sport, describes dressage simply as "the harmonious development of the physique and ability of the horse." Needless to say, any horse in any sport can benefit from an activity that develops his mind and body.

Certainly, skilled training in any sport can do this, but the basic movements of dressage, tested over four centuries, provide a solid foundation. So, many trainers and riders in all disciplines teach traditional dressage movements to both green horses and older horses, perfecting their skills. Dressage makes particular sense with older horses in retraining programs, since it provides such a good foundation for any athletic activity.

Foundation is the key word. Except for the seldom-performed exercises of classical *haute ecole*, the movements of dressage imitate nearly exactly the antics of a free, healthy, young horse. Horses at liberty collect themselves, extend, spin, and move laterally with flexible spines. Some will even do airs above ground worthy of the Spanish Riding School if they feel good enough about themselves.

Once a rider gets aboard a horse that has always been free, he imposes his weight and his decisions on the animal. The balance changes, the liberated attitude is suppressed, and the natural movements disappear. Dressage is a method used to bring back the gifts of nature to a horse that carries a rider. This is useful for any horse that is learning new skills, but a previously trained horse that has already had his natural movements altered dramatically will benefit the most.

Dressage will be especially important for horses like racing Thoroughbreds that were taught to do nothing but run fast and walk, and that were permitted to be stiff, hard-mouthed, and unresponsive. Nothing else mattered if he ran fast enough. It will be valuable for a former driving horse, whose loss of natural balance was different. He will

Horses of all breeds and backgrounds can benefit from training in dressage.

need to learn how to work in balance with a rider. And it will be useful for a Western-trained horse; although as you'll discover later, a carefully trained stock horse may already be able to perform many of the advanced movements.

Basic dressage training is also valuable for a horse and rider planning to compete in equitation events or riding-horse competitions, either Western or English. Events in which only the rider is judged, or in which the horse's overall usefulness is the only consideration, rarely call for specific dressage movements or principles. But a horse that moves like a dressage horse and responds to aids like a dressage horse will earn all the points he needs for a ribbon for himself or his rider.

Endurance horses, whose sport calls for no specific movements at all, benefit from dressage, too. They will learn to be less nervous and thereby expend less energy. Lengthened and extended gaits cover ground more efficiently. Flexibility helps with obstacles and tight turns. Dressage work will be invaluable for horses being retrained for any of these competitions.

Naczar, a fourteen-year-old Arab, began his working life as a Western horse. He moved on to endurance and after a couple of years of competition, came to Nancy Cole's Northern Lights Farm in Bethany, Connecticut. Cole, an event and dressage trainer, began working with Naczar to help his owner give him a dressage foundation. Naczar, while he quickly grasped the basics, was never expected to compete seriously in dressage. The schooling was to improve his overall endurance performance.

Other horses that come to Cole have no choice but to learn dressage. Eventing, in whatever form—pre-training-level trials that take one day or full three-day events—requires a dressage test. It's a specially written test that, in the three-day events, counts for less than 20 percent of the score. But it's true dressage, and the horse has to be able to do it to be competitive at any level in eventing. Event horses often come from other activities, almost never pure dressage, so many have to approach the dressage phase of eventing as an entirely new sport.

Finally, dressage itself may be your ultimate goal for your retrained horse. Sometimes horses intended initially for eventing may show no

Naczar, in only his second dressage lesson, is working to improve his endurance performances.

talent or proclivity for the cross-country part of the competition, which is so heavily weighted that it's often the first thing eventing competitors check in a new prospect. But the same horse may have the physical characteristics and mental attitude that make him suited for dressage. Eventing is forgotten and dressage becomes the goal.

Dressage prospects are also discovered in sports and breeds that don't normally supply prospects for the upper levels; although this happens less often in North America today than it did a few years ago. Today, a booming breeding and import industry in European warmbloods provides a good supply of horses bred for dressage.

In the past, American dressage competitors had to look a little harder for their prospects, even horses that were destined for the very highest levels. During the early 1980s, the eight Grand Prix finalists in one United States Dressage Championships consisted of an Appaloosa, a Quarter Horse, a Connemara-Thoroughbred cross, a

Percheron-Thoroughbred cross, a registered Thoroughbred, and three outnumbered warmbloods. Today, the non-warmbloods would probably be badly outnumbered at the top level.

But there are obviously still fine dressage prospects to be found among horses bred for other activities. Even though they may face a difficult challenge if the goal is to be the best dressage horse in the country, there are plenty of other levels of competitive dressage in which they can do well.

WHAT TO LOOK FOR IN A DRESSAGE RETRAINING PROSPECT

Almost every horse will benefit from learning dressage movements. And given enough time and adequate instruction, almost any horse can learn to do enough to perform through the lower levels. But some can learn more easily than others, and some can advance to the higher levels of the competitive sport.

CONFORMATION

When you consider a particular horse as a retraining prospect for dressage, you should look for certain characteristics. A horse lacking them will not be useless, but it will mean that you will have to work a little bit harder. Nancy Cole says that she looks first at the overall balance of the horse.

"I look for the same basic characteristics in a horse for any sport," she says. "I want a horse with four straight legs and four round feet. I want a horse that, when you look at him from the side, you can divide into three equal parts. The shoulder, the barrel, and the hip should be about in thirds."

Although balance is the ideal, as it is in most equine sports, there are some characteristics that might deviate from balance without damaging the horse's dressage potential. Slightly high withers, for example, help a horse transfer his weight off the forehand, a key to both the fluid movement and the perfect balance that are the goals of dressage.

High withers have another advantage. They often result from a deep shoulder, which helps a horse with both the lengthened strides required in the lower levels of dressage and the extensions required at the higher levels.

Horses whose withers and croup are the same height also are capable of shifting balance behind and often have sufficiently deep shoulders to extend. But horses with higher croups than withers may have serious problems.

"A horse built downhill is never going to have an easy time shifting his balance back onto his haunches," Cole says. "The biggest problem in collecting a horse comes when he's naturally built downhill."

The lowest levels of dressage competition do not require true collection, so a croup-high horse might manage some dressage, but only up to a point. He can, however, certainly benefit from the foundation of training.

Head carriage, often related to the shoulders and wither height, is another consideration. What to look for again depends on your goals in dressage. High head carriage contributes to the shape and balance required for advanced collection. But the lower levels, including the level necessary for eventing, will not require the kind of high head and extreme collection that the upper levels do.

"For the lower levels, it's important that you have a horse that can lengthen," Cole says. "At the higher levels, you might sacrifice some of the lengthening for a horse that can sit on its hocks and collect." So, you might look for a higher natural head carriage in a horse that you want to train for more advanced dressage than in a horse aimed at eventing or the lower levels.

The shape of the neck is important for successful dressage, but Cole points out that some necks may have been shaped by previous exercise rather than nature. The concave line of a ewe-neck, for example, would normally be highly undesirable in a dressage prospect.

"A ewe-neck is difficult if it's a result of the way a horse is built," she says. "But you frequently find a ewe-neck in a trained horse because he's never done the right work." A good training program in which the horse is required to flex the poll might fix the concave neck.

You will also take a close look at the prospect's legs, something you should do with any horse intended for any use. You want good legs in any sport, but the definition of good varies from sport to sport. In most disciplines, front leg conformation is most significant. In dressage, good front legs are important, but good hind legs are vital.

"The thing that I like the least in conformation for dressage is a very straight hind leg," Cole says. "This makes it very hard for [a] horse to bend the hock and step under. I like to see a good angle to the hind legs."

Since a horse with a fairly straight hind leg can often run fast and jump high, you may find yourself with a promising event prospect that's straight in the hocks. This horse may learn enough dressage to compete

A horse at liberty can demonstrate buoyant gaits and natural collection.

in eventing, but dressage will probably never be a good competition for him, even though true collection isn't part of the test.

Sometimes the occasional straight-hocked horse does well at the lower levels of dressage. A Thoroughbred with a long, low daisy-cutter stride may perform the lengthened strides of the lower-level tests in spite of straight hocks. He may never be able to produce the collection and elevated gaits needed for extreme collection, but he will do well in the lower levels and with the modest collection needed in the dressage phase of combined training.

Finally, some horses have naturally elevated gaits that translate well to the requirements of dressage. Naczar was such a horse.

"He had such natural buoyancy that he could go in the bridle immediately," Cole says. "He had the right topline initially."

Watching a horse at liberty will tell you something about the quality of his gaits, his physical balance, and any natural collection that he might enjoy. Even an untrained horse can show you characteristics that will make him a good dressage prospect.

ATTITUDE

When assessing a horse's potential for dressage, his mental attitude is as important as his conformation. Any horse except a true outlaw can learn some of the lower-level movements, but competitive dressage requires something special for success. The horse has to have an occasionally contradictory combination of personality traits that can be helped by training, but rarely created.

The horse must be absolutely obedient, yet active, forward, and enthusiastic about his work. Many absolutely obedient horses are dull and slow, and such an animal will never do well in dressage. On the other hand, an animated and active horse is often inclined to do precisely what he wants to at any given moment, exhibiting something less than absolute obedience. To excel at dressage, a horse has to balance the two characteristics.

In general, trainers prefer their horses to be a little spirited going into training, feeling that the training program itself will teach submission. Training can't add spirit to a dullard, but it can modify it in a horse that has a little too much.

Consider one more point about personality: A dressage horse is supposed to show no tension or resistance in his body or his actions. Some horses are deeply and intrinsically tense, and it's debatable whether they will live long enough to be trained out of showing tension, particularly if they are adult career changers.

A little tension won't matter in a horse that is learning dressage for his own improvement. It won't matter much in a brilliant steeplechaser that's going to do so well in his cross-country competition that his so-so dressage score won't keep him out of the medals. It will matter in a horse that is expected to compete in pure dressage, however, and you will have to assess the implications of putting time and perhaps money into a tense and nervous adult horse.

SADDLES

Even if you intend to use dressage for foundation training and never plan to compete, you will be wise to beg, borrow, or buy a dressage saddle. Other saddles, although they can be used, just won't allow the kind of contact between the rider and horse that is necessary for successful dressage work. They also discourage the rider from achieving the balance that permits the horse to move his center of balance off of his forehand.

Some forward-seat saddles used for jumping and hunter-style English riding on the flat can be used, but even the best of these, the deep-seated all-purpose saddle, encourages the rider to lean forward. That's their purpose, after all. The all-purpose places the rider a little further back than the jumping saddle, but it's hardly ideal in a sport in which you want the horse to carry his own weight back rather than forward.

The saddle-seat saddle, used by gaited-horse riders, may be appropriate in some ways for dressage, but it's probably even less ideal. The modern saddle-seat saddle is actually a descendent of the English show saddle of the nineteenth century that was used by European dressage riders during the first half of the twentieth century. The sport of dressage developed, primarily in Europe, before entirely appropriate tack appeared on the market.

The straight flaps of the modern show saddle do allow free shoulder movement, which is appropriate for dressage, and both the flat seat and the location of the stirrup bars force the rider to sit back. This allows collection to the rear and permits animated movement in front.

But the dressage saddle, developed in England after World War II, adds several other benefits. It features a deep, short seat which allows the rider to maintain a strong seat on the horse. There is a knee roll, similar to the one in the forward-seat saddle, which helps keep the upper leg and knee secure against the saddle. The bars sit back on the tree, positioning the stirrup leathers directly beneath the rider. The leathers themselves are long and straight, so the knee is well positioned to maintain lower-leg flexibility. The short girth keeps the buckles out of the way of the leg, and the rider can be very precise in the contact between boot and horse.

A dressage saddle requires proper placement of the rider's weight and legs.

While you can ride some dressage movements pretty well in a saddle-seat saddle, and you can execute a few in an all-purpose saddle, both are designed to do other things for the rider and the horse. Maintaining familiarity for the horse is no reason to avoid a dressage saddle. A horse moving to dressage from another sport probably won't notice any difference, because the change in the rider's center of balance is relatively small.

As with any change of equipment, start gradually. Increase the time of use as it becomes clear that the horse is working without soreness or discomfort.

BRIDLES

The standards of dressage require acceptance of the bridle and bit. Softness of the jaw is the key here. Softness can be both the cause and the result of bridle acceptance. The good dressage horse needs and accepts contact between the bit and the bars of his mouth, but it's a very short step between contact and pressure. It's also a short step in the other direction between contact and slackness. A horse with a bit that doesn't stay in one place will never be in constant contact, and the rider will have to either apply more pressure than is ideal or loosen up more than he should for good control.

Horses, particularly those that have had bad experiences in the past, discover all kinds of ways to move the bit around and avoid even, necessary contact. The easiest and favorite evasive step is the opening of the mouth, which allows the jaw to be crossed. Bit problems seem to be the rule rather than the exception among horses entering dressage work from other sports.

"I find most horses open their mouths too much," Nancy Cole says. "In many sports, it doesn't matter, but in dressage it does. I don't mind if they play with the bit a little, but not turn the bit to the side, cross their jaws, and ignore it."

Unfortunately, open mouths and the resulting evasion may have become a firmly entrenched habit in horses originally trained for other uses. Evasion is especially common in horses trained initially in big snaffles with plain raised nosebands, but it can happen quickly when a Western-trained horse is switched from a curb to a snaffle.

A noseband with a drop effect—either a simple dropped noseband or something more complex—puts pressure on the nose, lowering the head and forcing the horse to accept the direct contact of the bit on the bars. A Western-trained horse that was used in a bosal will have already experienced a similar effect of pressure on the nose, but the bosal bridle lacks a bit. He will accept the pressure but may object to the constant contact of the bit that the pressure causes.

Dressage trainers tend to use specialty nosebands when they work with horses that open their mouths too much, sliding their bits out of contact with their bars. These nosebands provide slightly different effects than the common drop noseband.

A common choice is the flash noseband, which combines a regular cavesson–type raised noseband with a device that produces a drop effect. It's either a second, lower noseband connected to the regular one or the old-fashioned style of two straps attached to the cavesson, crossed on top of the nose, then buckled underneath the jaw.

The flash exerts pressure where the two sections attach or cross, just below the cavesson. The pressure point is higher than that on the drop noseband, and the bridle is somewhat less severe as a result. If the flash is tightly buckled under the chin, severity is increased to the level of the drop, or even beyond.

The figure-eight noseband is another option for training. Horses that pull hard in addition to evading the bit—a characteristic of Thoroughbreds from the racetrack or horses previously ridden by heavy-handed people—may do well with the figure-eight, which lacks the raised cavesson. Instead, two straps cross on top of the nose and are connected under the jaw. The lack of the raised noseband means that more pressure is exerted on the point of crossing than with the flash, but it does permit more mobility for the horse's mouth, which improves jaw softness.

"How tightly you have to close the mouth depends on the horse," Cole says. "It's something that horses from other sports are usually

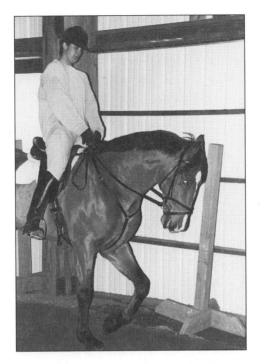

*A flash, or figure-eight, noseband
forces the horse to close his mouth and
encourages him to yield his jaw.*

not accustomed to, and I'm very careful initially. Some horses don't mind it at all when you put it on, but others won't go forward. I make sure the horse understands he still has to go forward before I close the mouth."

The specialty nosebands are always used with some kind of snaffle bit. But even a horse that doesn't need to have his mouth closed will probably begin his retraining in a snaffle. No matter what kind of bit he used in his previous career, he will have to be introduced to a snaffle so he can learn the kind of contact he will have to accept in dressage.

A simple, ringed, jointed snaffle is the common choice. Most well-trained horses, even Western horses, were started in them. See Chapter Four for information on introducing snaffles to the Western-trained horse that has never used one.

Eggbutt or D-ring snaffles can be used in training and may be effective on a horse that likes to slide the bit through his mouth in order to ignore it. And these bits also prevent the horse from playing with his bit, thereby loosening his jaw and teaching him not to fight the bit. You'll have to assess the habits your horse picked up in his previous career and make the decision based on them. When in doubt, go with the common loose-ringed snaffle.

The snaffle will remain the bit of choice for most horses being taught dressage as a foundation, or for one that is never expected to compete beyond the lower levels. Advanced horses will eventually be moved on to a Weymouth, with a snaffle, a curb, and a set of reins for each. The double bridle helps the horse obtain the body shape of extreme collection.

Some horses in other sports are ridden in double bridles, and yours may be experienced with one. But even if he's never worn one before, he may perform better because of his previous training. Some Western horses will be happy to respond to the familiar curb even after they learn to work with a snaffle.

The horse that never progresses to the Weymouth may still be trained in a more sophisticated bit than the snaffle. This is the pelham, a bit that features just one mouthpiece but two sets of rings and two sets of reins. This bit creates a snaffle effect when the rider raises his hands, and a curb effect when he lowers them. Previously trained adult horses often do well with the pelham.

Pelham bits—which include the single-reined kimberwicke—allow more precise work in collection and headset. They may be a good training choice for a horse that is benefiting from dressage but is not going to compete at the higher levels. Many horses trained originally for Western sports do particularly well with the kimberwicke.

STARTING DRESSAGE TRAINING

Preliminary dressage training has a goal that's both simple to explain and challenging to reach. Nancy Cole explains what you have to do to begin the retraining process.

"The first thing you want to teach him is to go forward from your leg in a straight and relaxed manner," she says. The problem with a previously trained horse is that he may never have been asked for these things, or, even worse, he may have been allowed to get away with just the opposite.

"I find that horses who have done other sports or who haven't been trained systematically have to learn to go forward from your leg, which they often have never really felt," Cole says. "They have to accept your leg and not scoot out or go faster. Make them keep the same rhythm."

This can be a challenge to a horse that learned that pressure from his rider's legs means either a faster version of the same gait or a faster gait. In dressage, he will have to understand that strong forward movement and impulsion are not the same things as speed.

The first step is to make sure you keep steady hands. "Don't drop the contact with the bit," Cole says. "You want the horse to go long and low at first, but you have to maintain contact."

But how about the rounded shape of dressage? Trying for that too early can prevent the horse from learning to go forward.

"Frequently I find people trying to teach their horses to go forward with a round neck, but first they have to go forward with a long neck," Cole says. "The short neck comes later, with collection from the back."

Part of going forward is the willingness of the horse to reach for the bit and stretch the neck out to do it. Casually trained horses may have never done this, nor have Western-trained horses that used only curb bits, never snaffles. These horses will assume that leg means faster.

In accepting impulsion without speed, the horse learns to accept contact with his mouth at the same time that leg pressure is applied. The consistent combination makes him understand that the two signals are not contradictory.

The concept is simple. Apply leg aids to urge the horse forward while maintaining steady hands. It's a delicate balance. When the horse responds to the leg by moving forward, a reduction in bit contact will tell him to go faster. This is what he expects, and if you ease too much he will indeed go faster rather than stronger. On the other hand, if you fight this natural inclination and increase contact, the signal will tell the horse to shorten strides, to slow down, or both.

This problem with maintaining balance will exist with any horse being given his preliminary dressage lessons, but it will be especially apparent in previously trained horses. Increasing and decreasing contact were half of his cue—along with leg pressure—to go faster or slower. He will not understand the concept of keeping the same speed with greater impulsion, so you will have to be particularly careful with your hands. The give-and-take for pace does exist in dressage, so he won't have to forget the concept. But he will have to learn something new.

As he develops the ability to move forward, he's encouraged to stretch and reach for the bit by the rider combining steady and gentle leg pressure with the steady and gentle contact with the bit. Learning the concept of moving forward from the leg may take some time, depending on how firmly entrenched the horse's previous habits were. If he seems reluctant and upset by the combination of aids, try asking him to go forward while reaching for the bit for only a few strides, then ease off the leg pressure. You should be able to steadily increase the length of time that he accepts the leg and bit.

Relaxation is the next challenge. A certain level of relaxation will come naturally as the horse has successful experiences in his retraining process. A horse that appears tense as you begin to work with him may be tense because he's unfamiliar with new tack and new demands.

Horses whose nervousness is more firmly entrenched need extra patience, calmness, and quiet handling on your part—but they don't need to be allowed to get away with less work. They often need to have exercises repeated long after they master them, even to the point of boredom. A bored horse is not a tense one.

It also helps to ask the tense or nervous horse to slow down to a walk and to stop. Move on again, then slow. This procedure helps calm edgy horses.

Some horses spook or jump around out of youth or high spirits rather than nervousness. Although they can't be allowed to get away with less work either, they usually don't need to be punished.

"As much as possible I ignore it," Nancy Cole says. "The more attention you pay to it, the more it becomes a big deal. If the horse does something stupid, I just keep on with what I'm doing and ignore it." Serious misbehavior has to be corrected immediately, but occasional little hops or spooks shouldn't require anything more than continued application of the aids that were being used when the horse made his move.

Once the horse understands the principle of going forward from the leg in a relaxed manner, he can move on to the final aspect of the three-part goal of preliminary dressage training—straightness. This is a goal that seems simple, but can be very difficult to reach.

"Most horses coming out of other sports are not truly straight," Cole says. Horses tend to favor one side or the other naturally, because of conformation, soundness, habit, or a combination of factors. One-sidedness is also imposed by particular sports.

Racehorses go counterclockwise. They do jog and even canter a little in the opposite direction, but very few enjoy the kind of training facilities that allow them to work seriously turning right. Most other sports call for horses to work in both directions, but training facilities often encourage work in one direction. Lazy trainers also permit horses to work more often in the direction that they prefer.

A previously trained horse most likely worked under unevenly distributed weight, and this will probably have caused muscle development and body carriage that favors that direction. These horses will have to be worked in exercises to overcome this as they progress in dressage, but in the early lessons it will be enough to be aware of the problem and to make sure that the horse works in both directions equally.

CONTINUED TRAINING

As the horse continues his dressage training, he should be expected to improve in the basics before he's expected to learn specific dressage exercises. Forward movement is the most important of the basics and, for some horses, may be what is keeping him from progressing adequately in his new sport.

Impulsion is both an important part of basic training and a vital foundation for the advanced exercises. Forward movement is equally important for extended and collected gaits. Its importance is obvious in extension, but it may be even more important in collection, since the impression of controlled power simply doesn't exist without forward impulsion.

Impulsion is made part of a horse's normal way of going by repetition of consistent aids. Teaching the horse to go forward is, Nancy Cole says, the part of early dressage training that you can't hurry.

"It's the most important step," she says. "It's also the simplest. Unfortunately, it's the most boring. The horse is never allowed to get behind your leg. Never."

Horses from various sports may react more or less to the leg than you expect, and you will have to adjust your aids accordingly. A Thoroughbred off the racetrack may have never felt a leg at all, and the slightest squeeze will send him out too strongly. A horse originally trained in driving will also have felt no leg in his original career, although he presumably will have been introduced to leg aids as he was retrained to ride. But a horse coming out of Western performance events will have been subjected to strong leg aids and may pay little attention to yours.

A few lucky horses received good training in their initial sports and need little specific training to respond to dressage leg aids. Naczar was such a horse.

"He was well trained by a professional in his first sport, so he knew the leg, and he knew how to go forward," Cole says.

But she adds that even a horse that responds well sometimes needs a little extra emphasis. "We ride all our horses in spurs," she says. "If you have a bare boot and you ask them to go forward, but they don't, you have a problem."

As you continue dressage work with your retrained horse you may find that you rarely let up entirely on leg aids. This is particularly the case with a horse that has come out of Western events. The horse may let up on his forward impulsion as soon as you do. But the constant application of strong leg aids can lead to another problem.

Naczar learned in his previous career how to go forward from the leg, and he continues to do it now.

Some horses, used to a reduction of pressure once they've responded correctly, resent a rider who never relents. There is the danger of teaching the horse to ignore the leg, since he's going to feel it regardless of what he does. You should make sure you reward him a little—easing up just until he eases up on his impulsion—when he does what you ask.

If it's hard to reach a balance between too little and too much leg with your horse, you can add back and seat cues. To be sure, your back and seat muscles tighten naturally when you press your calf. But you can increase the signal by intentionally tightening your muscles a little more and deepening your seat in the saddle. It's a cue to drive forward that most horses seem to instinctively understand, and it's very useful with horses that respond poorly to leg pressure. Unfortunately, it's hard on the rider's back.

Some horses need combined vigorous aids for at least a short period in order to grasp the concept of forward impulsion, but once they do, you should be able to employ a reasonable combination of leg aids and slight muscle tightening to maintain the movement.

Some trainers rely on schooling whips to reinforce impulsion and to encourage an even pace. Others believe that, given the suddenness of its application, the whip has the opposite effect. Unlike legs and seat, if it is constantly applied it will turn into punishment or even torture. Still others will use a schooling whip occasionally, but they rely primarily on plenty of sessions in the ring with vigorous use of the legs.

Part of proper impulsion is control of the pace, since the horse can't be allowed to jump forward when the leg is applied. This requires steady contact through the reins, which won't be a problem for most English-trained horses. You may discover that a Western-trained horse, unless he was originally trained in a snaffle or has had a long period of basic retraining, may have difficulty adjusting to the contact. These horses may need slightly less contact at first, although less contact does not mean a loose rein. Gradually increase the contact to the level you will need for him to be adequately on the bit.

A horse struggling with impulsion shouldn't be forced to maintain the movement you want for more than a few minutes while he's still struggling. Between successful periods of impulsion, rest him (and yourself, since it's hard work). Rest doesn't mean letting the horse revert to sloppy stop-and-go gaits. It means a break, followed by more work on impulsion.

Continued training also means more work on relaxation. The body in general, and the jaw in particular, have to be soft and relaxed in order to continue on to the more difficult work in dressage. It's inevitable that a horse new to dressage, especially one new to almost every aspect of it, will be tense at times.

You will probably be able to feel muscle tension beneath you as you ride. Someone watching you ride the horse will also notice. The way the horse uses his tail is a good indication of body tension or relaxation.

"The horse who carries his tail nice and relaxed and out from his body reflects how soft and straight his spine is," Cole says. "If he clamps his tail or pulls it off to one side, it's an indication of tension in the body."

When the tension remains after the horse understands the basics of his new responsibilities, it may indicate a physical problem. Take time at this point to check his tack for fit and to examine his mouth for soreness on the bars or irritation at the side of the mouth. Have his feet checked, too. Some unsoundness doesn't show up with a limp.

It's not uncommon for a horse that is going through a career change to develop physical problems because of unfamiliar tack, different shoeing, or some other change. The problems tend to show up after a few weeks of work, as soon as the changed equipment has had a chance to irritate him.

Tension in the body may also be a reaction to the unfamiliar strenuousness of the driving aids. Even if the horse seems to be responding properly, you may have to alter the aids if they are preventing him from relaxing.

Try more seat and less leg, or more leg and less seat, or a different balance. You may have to experiment to find the combination that makes the horse mentally and physically comfortable. Only a comfortable horse can truly relax.

A relaxed body leads to a relaxed jaw, and many horses will effortlessly improve in the jaw as they become comfortable with their training programs. But a horse that remains reluctant to yield his jaw to bit contact may need a change of bit, a change of bridle, a change of hands, or all three.

A horse that, in his previous career, had been ridden in a severe bit by a heavy-handed rider may have learned to stiffen his jaw in resistance. Even the addition of a noseband to close the mouth often does little to prevent a skilled jaw-tightener from resisting the bit. It's a well-established pattern that takes work to break.

Usually, a very mild snaffle combined with one of the drop-style nosebands will work. Try a figure-eight if the flash doesn't work, or a plain drop if neither of the others work.

Sometimes, the hard-jawed horse got that way because he was ridden in a mild, loose snaffle that he learned to control, either by getting his tongue over the top of it or by sliding it out of his way. One of the drop-style nosebands should work here, too. But this horse may need a slightly more severe bit, perhaps one with a port that will keep his tongue in place.

No matter what caused his bit evasion in the past, he may have developed head and neck muscles to help him stiffen against the bit. Proper training will soften the unwanted muscles and develop the ones that he needs. Also useful will be continued work on the third part of basic training: straightness.

Straightness may be the most difficult of the three basic skills to teach. While it's relatively easy to make a horse go more or less straight, absolute straightness is something else entirely.

"True straightness is very hard to achieve," Cole says. "It's something you can work on all your life."

Straightness in dressage is maintained the same way that it is in other sports, by adjusting rein contact depending on the direction the horse is traveling and by the position of the leg to keep the hindquarters in line. Any horse that was used in a sport that includes leg aids will understand and respond. But most other sports are not nearly so particular about straightness as dressage, and the horse may never have had it demanded of him at more than a minimal level.

The rail is both a blessing and a curse in working on straightness. On the one hand, the side rails of a ring provide an obvious parallel to work against. But a ring is rarely big enough to provide more than a few strides of absolutely straight line.

"Don't always stay on the rail," Cole advises. "You can deceive yourself about how straight your horse is, and you can end up using the rail as your outside aids. Use the quarter lines instead."

Continued work will help a horse become comfortable going forward in a straight manner, but traveling up and down a quarter line will only do so much to overcome the natural tendencies against straightness.

"In order to put a horse absolutely straight, you have to be able to bend him equally left and right," Cole says. "When the horse is ready, you develop exercises for lateral movement—the shoulder in, haunches in, leg yield—which you must make the horse perform equally on both sides."

LATERAL MOVEMENTS

The lateral dressage exercises are not just the key to straightness. Some are also important movements in intermediate dressage tests. What's more, they lead on in natural progression to the advanced movements.

It's beyond the scope of this book to teach a reader how to train a horse in dressage movements. You will need a live instructor for that. But you will see here some of the points that you—or your instructor—should keep in mind if your horse came out of another sport.

The lateral movements, the first complex exercises the dressage horse is asked to perform, are also called two-track movements, since the forelegs and hind legs make separate tracks. No other equine sport calls for precisely the same group of movements, but some feature a few near matches. If your horse was Western-trained and was used in cutting or Western riding competitions he may be able to do several of the dressage lateral movements. He won't look exactly the same, and he will need slightly different signals, but he should be able to do them. If he was simply well-trained by a Western professional, he may also be able to do some of the lateral movements.

The leg yield is the first lateral movement taught in dressage, and a nearly identical movement, usually called the two-track, is taught as a basic skill by good Western trainers. The leg yield is a valuable training exercise in dressage because it helps improve suppleness, flexibility, and balance. It's not a difficult movement, and it doesn't do as much good for the horse as some of the more complex lateral movements, but it's an important and necessary first step.

In Western training it's useful as a basic skill, necessary for Western riding horses and absolutely vital for cutting horses that use it to follow the movement of the cow while keeping her directly in front of them. In both the leg yield and the two-track, the horse's body is straight but angled in relation to the direction the horse is traveling. In a movement to the right, the right fore- and hind legs cross in front of the left fore- and hind legs.

In cutting and Western riding, several slightly different moves are often referred to simply as two-tracking, although some Western train-ers do train for and identify distinct movements. In dressage, the pro-gressively more difficult lateral exercises will always be given individual names, like shoulder in, haunches in, or haunches out.

The most extreme of the lateral movements always gets its own name in Western use. The sidepass, called the full pass or full travers in dressage, is required in Western riding competitions and can be done in cutting if rider and horse are lucky enough to get a cow that asks for it. A good sidepass exhibition will always help a cutting horse win.

The sidepass and the full pass are basically the same movement, with the horse required to move sideways, his legs crossing over and in front of each other. The Western riding sidepass often becomes more complicated, with poles, barriers, and platforms sometimes inserted into the exercise.

You will occasionally find horses from other sports that can do a respectable sidepass or full pass, too. The movement helps a horse line up properly at the end of a show class, and a meticulous trainer may have taught it to any horse.

There are great similarities between the two-track movements in Western and dressage use, and most of the aids are identical. But there are important differences.

The direction of the front end is determined by the reins, while the rear end is directed by the legs. Leg aids are usually the same in both sports, but rein cues are not, and you must keep this in mind as you con-vert the Western horse's two-track and sidepass to the dressage horse's lateral exercises.

First, consider the leg aids. In both sports, a lateral movement to the left calls for leg pressure on the right behind the girth to move the hindquarters right. The left leg on or near the girth helps maintain direction and impulsion.

In dressage, the rein signal for a leg-yield move to the left consists of increased pressure on the left rein to ask for a move in that direction. In some lateral exercises—the leg yield is one—the head is bent slightly away from the direction of movement, so there will be a little right rein as well. Firm bit contact is maintained throughout.

In Western riding, the horse will have received neck-rein cues during his two-track work. Even a horse that was trained initially on a snaffle will have almost always done lateral movements with a curb, and that means he will have worked with very little contact. The rein signal for the two-track is a movement of both reins to the direction of movement. This creates the neck-rein signal on the opposite side.

The rein signals of the two styles are not quite as different as they seem. In dressage, contact is maintained, but the rein signals are less important than leg cues in the lateral movements. In Western riding, the horses are neck-reined into the lateral movements, but there is a little direct-rein contact on the opposite side to create the bend of the head.

Other movements of intermediate dressage appear in one form or another in cutting, reining, working cow-horse competition, and Western riding events. The spin, rollback, flying change of lead, and other movements have their parallels in dressage. If you're unfamiliar with Western competition events, attend a few stock-horse shows to see what the movements look like when well performed. You will be able to judge for yourself their similarities and differences.

In most cases, a horse that knows the Western movements will easily learn the dressage equivalents. You may find that the quickest and easiest method of developing dressage-style exercises in a horse that knows the Western movements is to neck rein the horse at first, then gradually switch him to the English direct rein. *Gradual* is relative. It can often be done in one session, although some horses will need several lessons. See Chapter Four for information on the procedure to be followed in teaching a neck-reining horse to direct rein.

*Extreme collection will be required of horses only at
the highest levels of dressage.*

There are many other steps in dressage, including extreme collection and extension. Some horses are not physically or mentally capable of these body shapes and movements, and most riders aren't interested in pursuing dressage to that level. If you are, consider advanced training for you and your horse.

Also ahead of you will be the unique dressage movements like the piaffe and passage. By the time the retrained horse is ready to learn these skills, his previous training will probably play a very small part in how he learns. He will be a fully qualified dressage horse by then.

CHAPTER NINE

Jumping

EXPERTS DISAGREE ON WHETHER HORSES ACTUALLY like to jump or whether any horse over the age of six months will do it, given a choice of going over or around.

Some people are convinced that horses don't like to jump. After all, most horses don't hop over their pasture fences, even if there is green and succulent grass on the other side. The world's oldest breeds, Arabs and the primitive coldbloods of Asia, don't usually jump very well, suggesting that early horses seldom did it.

Those who are convinced that horses like to jump point out that most horses can do it a little and some can do it remarkably well. Since we can only observe, and not question, we don't really know.

Ultimately it doesn't really matter if horses like to jump, because people who ride horses most emphatically do. It's a thrilling and exhilarating activity—more exciting for most riders than racing or any other equine sport.

During the lifetime of almost every non-draft horse, someone will wonder whether he might be able to jump. Many will never actually be asked to do it, since they may be doing just fine in their original careers. But many will indeed be tried over fences.

The ability to jump is not limited to horses of particular breeds or types. Even draft horses can jump a little, if they're asked. Eventing trainer Nancy Cole believes horses do jump naturally.

"Most horses are not afraid to jump," she says. "They will jump very readily. It's the minute we put weight on them and we start to ride that we can ruin their athletic ability."

Horses that come to jumping from other sports may have had their natural balance altered, their attitude soured, and their legs injured. Even so, most horses can learn to jump well, though it may take some longer than others.

"If your horse is sound and has a good attitude, he can be taught to jump three feet," Cole says. "Most people don't really need to jump higher than that."

Horses of any size and conformation can learn to jump, but some can do it more successfully and more safely than others. It's difficult to figure out just what makes some horses jump well and others not. When you're looking at a candidate for retraining as a jumper, you can find all the right characteristics and still choose the wrong horse. If you retrain a horse you already have in spite of the fact that he has all the wrong characteristics, he may prove to be just right. There's a certain mystery to jumping ability.

Still, some common qualities appear in horses that jump well, and other characteristics show up in horses that have problems jumping. Whenever possible, choose the horse most likely to be able to jump well, but don't be surprised if you're wrong.

As Nancy Cole points out, "I've had horses sent to me to train that I would never have bought myself. But they do just fine. For every rule, there are many exceptions."

First, consider size. Some Grand Prix riders will say they won't even look at a horse under 16.3 hands, since their courses demand horses that can jump enormous fences with vast spreads. This rule ignores Touch of Class, the only double Olympic-gold-medal winner of recent decades, who might have stood 16.1 on her tiptoes.

The less exceptional Grand Prix horses (if such a thing exists as an unexceptional Grand Prix competitor) may have to be big, given the demands of their level of the sport, but many much smaller horses can jump far higher than most riders want to try. A 14-hand Quarter Horse once held the world high-jump record at just over eight feet.

In fact, some ponies jump remarkably well, possibly because they have less body weight to hoist over fences and usually carry lighter riders. Choose your jumping prospect according to the weight and size of the rider he's expected to carry and, to a slightly lesser extent, the height and scope of the jumps intended for him.

Other useful physical characteristics are strong, square hindquarters to help propel the horse over the obstacle, deep shoulders, and a back that isn't too long to remain sound with the regular body concussion caused by landing. Most important, though, are the legs.

Nancy Cole says a prospect you're planning to buy should be thoroughly vetted, since jumping is so taxing on the legs. "It's important that the vet understand that you plan to jump," she says.

"You must avoid horses with sore front feet and horses with knee problems," she advises. If a horse has become unsound in front in other sports, there is no way he will be sound enough to jump, given the far greater stress in the front legs that he will experience in his new sport.

Pay closest attention to the feet. "I'm a fanatic about front feet," Cole says. "I want a nice, round front foot with enough heel. It's also very important to me that both front feet are the same."

Hindquarters and legs are also important, but you have more flexibility there. "Back-end problems seem to be a lot more manageable," Cole says. "You can develop a horse behind in his soft tissue so he can compensate for a joint problem."

The feet should be of reasonable size to support the body. That means big feet for a big horse and small feet for a smaller horse. A horse with feet too big for his body, a situation sometimes seen in draft-horse crosses used for driving, will probably have trouble folding up his front legs going over fences. A horse with feet too small for his body weight, often seen in stock horses shown in hand, will have trouble staying sound once those little feet experience the concussion of jumping.

Horses coming off the racetrack are infamous for leg problems. In general, racing Thoroughbreds have more front-leg unsoundness, while Standardbreds have a lot of hock problems. Each breed can also suffer from the other problem, of course, so thoroughly examine all four legs of a former racehorse before attempting to jump.

In jumping, as in most sports, backs that are too long are usually more subject to injury than backs that are too short, but a long-backed horse in good proportion ought to be able to stay sound as a jumper. He may also be more flexible than the short-backed one, an important consideration if you plan to jump in competitions in which tight turns are important. On the other hand, a short-backed horse—perhaps a stock horse—will have the room to carry a rider in a jumping saddle, while he may lack the proper room for a saddle in a sport in which it carries the rider further back towards the hindquarters.

The horse's strides can also provide some clues. Horses with naturally high knee action are often likely to fold up well over a jump, but a horse with extremely bouncy action may lack the kind of rear-end impulsion necessary to get himself up and over an obstacle. A good striding horse should jump well, but what constitutes a good stride may be difficult to determine. A horse that's fairly careful in his strides will have an easier time placing himself in proper position to jump, but a free-striding horse will probably do better over long, low fences, cross-country, and on the hunting field.

Successful and safe jumping requires a good attitude. That's a combination of a willingness to be controlled and a lack of timidity. Some horses are simply not bold enough to risk themselves by going over a fence. Some timid horses can learn confidence, but some will always be afraid.

Other horses are bold, but they are unwilling to listen to a rider and can't be safely aimed at a fence. This may be trained out of them, but a little tendency to rebelliousness will probably always be lurking in the horse's personality.

It's hard to know how a horse will react to jumping unless you actually try him, but you can get some ideas with a short ride on the flat. A horse that shows unreasonable fear of his surroundings or one whose rebellion is relentless is not a good candidate for jumping.

EQUIPMENT

You can jump a horse in any kind of saddle. Seemingly improbable ones like sidesaddles and Western saddles can be used to jump. Until this century, ladies would complete twenty-mile hunt courses featuring dozens of demanding jumps while sitting on a sidesaddle in voluminous skirts. Even today, sidesaddle enthusiasts jump stadium courses and race through cross-country runs.

Western riders also jump. A Western rider who encounters an obstacle on the trail is going to take the quickest way across. The shortest route is usually a jump, which can be managed safely in a saddle with a low, roping-style horn. It's more of a challenge in a saddle with a high horn, but even then it can be done.

But no matter what the horse's previous experience, you will want to use a forward-seat saddle when you train him for jumping. It's easiest on the horse and most secure for the rider.

There are variations in flap length and shape, seat length and depth, stirrup-bar placement, and knee rolls. Trainers and riders debate which style is best for which jumping sport. Your choice will depend on the amount of jumping versus the amount of flat riding your activity entails.

The forward-seat jump saddle is ideal for jumping, but less than ideal for riding on the flat. The modern all-purpose saddle moves the rider a little further back and may be initially more comfortable for a horse or rider used to a Western saddle or a saddle-seat saddle. It's better than the jump saddle for riding on the flat, but not quite as effective over the jumps.

With the majority of horses, you may feel free to use the saddle most suited to the activity. Most are comfortable and move freely at the fast canter and gallop with the rider's weight balanced over or just behind the withers. A few inches either way won't matter. The sensation of either kind of forward-seat saddle may be slightly unfamiliar, but neither interferes with the horse's action behind.

Some previously trained horses may need a longer period of adjustment. One that seems unbalanced or awkward in a jumping saddle may do better in the all-purpose saddle during the early days of jump training. By the time he's ready for bigger jumps and longer training sessions he should be well-adjusted to the shift of the rider's weight and will be comfortable in a pure jumping saddle.

In the past, most saddles suitable for jumping were comparatively narrow, designed primarily for Thoroughbreds or Thoroughbred crosses. A wider-backed horse, such as a Quarter Horse, a Morgan, or an

Arab, might prove difficult to fit. Today, most large tack shops carry jumping saddles with wider trees, mostly to accommodate warmbloods. They may be suitable for horses being retrained from other sports too.

As with any change of saddle, the horse will need careful fitting, appropriate padding, and regular checks to prevent and treat any irritations that develop. Minor problems are almost inevitable with a saddle that places weight and pressure in unfamiliar spots. Pay extra attention to the withers and the back of the shoulder, because a horse coming out of another sport might have used saddles with cantle and flaps cut much further back than those on jumping saddles.

BITS AND BRIDLES

Most horses will be taught to jump in a simple snaffle bit, but they may later progress to the single bar, double-reined pelham, which provides a snaffle plus mild-curb effect. Some jumpers move on to a full double

Buddy, with his snaffle and flash noseband, is ready to respond to the rider's hands without fighting the contact.

*Some horses respond well to a shadow roll, which
prevents them from noticing distractions under their feet.*

bridle, but this would never be used on a horse learning to jump for the
first time.

A plain, ringed snaffle will suit the vast majority of horses that are
beginning to jump. Even one coming out of a curb-bit sport—Western
or gaited competitions, for example—should be tried first in a mild
snaffle.

Successful jumping requires nearly continuous, sometimes strong,
contact to modify pace into a jump, and the Western horse in particular might not be willing to go forward on steady contact, even with a
familiar bit. Once he learns the snaffle effect, he may be changed to a
pelham or double bridle if he really needs a curb. You may even consider
a gag, rare in modern jumping until Touch of Class won an Olympic
gold medal wearing one. But the snaffle comes first.

A horse that opens his mouth too much may need a flash, figure-eight, or dropped noseband, as may a horse that clenches his jaw and ignores his rider's rein signals. Pace and straightness cannot be properly regulated if the horse is the one in control of the bit.

Some trainers and riders of jumping horses use shadow rolls on or sometimes above the noseband to prevent the horse from seeing sights below their front feet that might make them spook, run out, or just take a distracting look. Many racehorses, especially Standardbreds that competed at raceways at night, feel comfortable and secure with shadow rolls, although many more wear them than actually need them.

Some nonspooky racehorses, coming out of the barn of a trainer who always used shadow rolls, learn to expect their presence and become spooky without them. Consider using one on a former racehorse if he seems distracted by what's in front of him for no reason.

OTHER EQUIPMENT

Running martingales are commonly used on jumpers. They work very well on horses that resist the bit and charge fences. Horses that are entering jumping from other sports may have competed or trained in martingales, and they won't be surprised by the confinement if you choose to use one.

Unfortunately, horses that raced on the flat—often the animals most likely to pull and charge—will never have performed in a running martingale and almost as certainly never trained in one. Some Thoroughbreds don't deal well with confining equipment, even under the best of circumstances, so introducing a running martingale to a former racehorse should be done carefully and gradually.

Standardbred racehorses don't use running martingales either, but most of them use so much other head-setting equipment that the addition of a martingale shouldn't create much rebellion. Most jump trainers don't add a martingale of any kind until a horse has successfully completed his first jumps over small fences. This delay is even more important with a horse that is used to having a free head while working.

Most trainers bandage and boot horses during the early days of jump training, and some continue protection throughout the horse's jumping career. There is debate about just how protective the boots should be, since some people like horses to feel raps on the rails. People who subscribe to this think that a horse that touches a rail will learn to jump more cleanly next time.

Most beginning jumpers will need boots, wraps, or both, since the initial lessons should give the horse positive experiences, not bruises and leg pain. Some previously trained horses will have worn bandages and boots, although probably not the kind of ankle boots suitable for jumping.

Western horses may have worn bandages to compete in performance events, and some may have used bell boots, skid boots, and splint boots. Standardbreds might have been four-legged tack catalogues, wearing most protective devices known to the modern horseman. Racing Thoroughbreds would have worn bandages only, and then only if they had questionable soundness. Consider the previous sport and its equipment as you decide how much time you need to introduce protective equipment to a new jumper.

THE TRAINING PROGRAM

Horses new to jumping should start at the beginning of the training process; although the beginning for a previously trained horse is presumably further along than the beginning for a young, green one. Each step of the process should be shorter, unless the horse developed such bad habits in his former sport that he has to work harder to overcome them than he would to develop good ones in the first place.

FREE JUMPING

Trainers argue about whether it's a good idea to teach a horse to jump without a rider on his back. This is most often done on the lunge line, but trainers lucky enough to have a lot of space, patience, and friends can use a loose jumping arena, usually called a Hitchcock pen.

The trainer, lunge whip in hand and surrounded by as many friends as he can summon, urges the horse to jump obstacles inside the enclosed space. It's difficult to make the horse do and even more difficult to make him do it at the controlled pace necessary to reach the jumps at the right spot. But a trainer in possession of the proper-sized pen and a cooperative horse can observe the animal's form over fences and see how well he does in making decisions for himself.

Using a lunge line to ask for the jump gives more control and is usually easier on horse and trainer. But, according to opponents of jumping a horse without a rider, it's not an effective way to teach a horse the balance and propulsion that he will need to be a successful jumper.

Fortunately, most previously trained horses don't need to begin their training over jumps without a rider. They are almost always fully adult, and their legs and skeletons are mature enough to carry a rider's weight. A horse not yet sound enough to be ridden over jumps, possibly one just off the racetrack, isn't sound enough to jump, period.

GROUND WORK

Lungeing on the flat is useful for mature horses that are learning to jump. The horse will have to maintain steady pace within a gait and smooth transitions to faster gaits if he's going to be able to manage a jump course. Lungeing can provide training in pace control in a way that's simple and nonthreatening to the horse.

Nancy Cole concentrates on ridden work with previously trained horses. Even so, transitions between gaits are vital to success over jumps and are a major part of the prejumping training.

"I do lots and lots of transitions, at all three gaits," she says. "It's very important that the horse learns to hold his balance in the transitions. It's just as important that he doesn't get scared in the transition up to canter. You don't want him to have to worry about being on the wrong lead or being unbalanced."

Before moving on to training over obstacles, many horses coming out of other sports need to work on moving forward on leg cues. Buddy, a horse of unknown age and uncertain breeding, was sent to Cole's training center to be developed into an eventer. He had come out of an auction and, at the age of about ten, didn't know much about anything except carrying a rider.

"He was very willing. His problem was that he didn't understand the leg," Cole says. "He didn't understand how to stay straight. He would panic about things because he just didn't understand what was expected of him."

Buddy, with his owner hoping that he could become an eventer, had to learn dressage anyway. But even if he had been intended solely to jump, the dressage basics of going forward and straight from the leg were a major part of his learning to jump correctly.

"Until the horse stays reliably ahead of your leg, he will not jump safely," Cole says. "His basic education has to be that good."

So it was work on the flat for Buddy. He was asked to move forward smoothly from the leg, with bit contact preventing him from leaping forward when he felt leg pressure and lurching into transitions when asked to.

POLES

Buddy had jumped a little in his previous life, but since he needed work in regulating his gaits under leg urging, Cole chose to begin him over trotting poles, as she would have with a young horse.

Exercise over poles is valuable for every horse preparing to jump. It's a necessity for young horses that need both regulation of their gaits and experience in making decisions about when to pick up their feet.

It's useful in adult horses whose previous training may have been incomplete or that may have been allowed to develop sloppy strides. A horse extremely well-schooled in his previous sport may be able to skip work over poles or complete the work in a few minutes in one lesson.

The young horse will spend some time working on walking over poles first, but an adult horse may be able to move directly to trotting over a course of poles. A very clumsy adult horse might need some time walking, but if he's so clumsy that he can't walk over poles, he will probably have to be trained as if he were a green horse anyway.

Trotting poles help pace and give confidence to a horse prior to his first jump.

Cole does as much work over poles as the individual horse needs. "I will spend hours trotting poles, until they learn to pick up their feet. I use several poles, about four feet apart. Trotting poles may take three days [with] a horse that's never jumped."

Trotting poles helps a horse learn to keep his pace even, but it also serves to calm a horse that might become afraid at the sight of an obstacle. Poles on the ground won't scare many horses, and since they're easily negotiated at a simple trot, the process helps to give a horse confidence.

A Western-trained horse that has been used in Western riding or trail-horse competitions will have had plenty of experience with poles on the ground, but in his sport he will have been asked to pick his way through complicated or unusual patterns of objects on the ground, usually at the walk. He won't be afraid of going over obstacles, but he won't do it at a lively gait except with considerable urging. He may need more than three days of poles to develop good forward motion over the little obstacles.

During the pole-trotting process, the horse should be making his own decisions about stride. The rider works only to maintain strong forward movement and straightness.

"If you help them too much, you're not doing them any favors," Cole says. "You have to let them help themselves if they're going to learn."

With a series of poles four feet apart (more for a larger-than-average horse or less for a small one) the horse should be able to keep up a good, brisk trot with his feet hitting the ground in the middle of each space. Once he can do that repeatedly while maintaining forward impulsion, he can move on to the next step.

The best way for a horse to learn to jump is with a simple grid, starting with a trotting pole and a low cross rail.

GRIDS

"I start all my horses jumping with a very simple grid," Cole says. "A single jump allows the horse to make decisions about where they have to leave the ground. They don't really learn to jump with me placing them at the jump."

She always starts with a trotting pole on the ground, then adds a simple, very low cross rail. "The cross rail is just a couple of inches off the ground," she says. "I place it about nine feet from the pole."

The cross rail, although low, looks like a real jump, since it appears higher than it actually is at the center cross point. The crossed rails also help a horse stay straight over the jump, which is an important consideration even during the early days of learning to jump. The horse may have come out of activities in which performing straight was neither required nor particularly admired. The horse may have come to believe that you follow the cow rather than the straight line in front of you, or that you come around the far turn and angle into the rail. But he will have to learn to stay straight over jumps, even if he's later taught to take shortcuts between jumps.

This low initial jump is usually taken at a trot. Most horses are far more comfortable and secure at a trot than a canter, and most riders are less likely to interfere with the horse's mouth or balance at the slower gait. Not all horses are good trotters, however, and some might not do well being asked to jump out of a trot.

Western horses may never have been asked for a brisk trot. The Western jog is a much more leisurely gait. They may need more work over poles or even trotting on the flat with lots of leg before attempting to jump out of a trot. Trotting Standardbreds sometimes have too strong a trot or too great a determination to stay at the trot, and they may quickly show you that they're not quite ready to jump a fence out of a trot.

Pacing Standardbreds are another problem entirely. A natural pacer probably wouldn't have gotten over the trotting poles anyway, but if you believe you're ready to jump, and he's still pacing, see Chapter Six for suggestions on converting him to the trot.

Buddy is relaxed and confident over the cross rail of his grid.

The horse that's trotting strongly can be taken over the pole and the cross rail several times before another obstacle is added. "I put in a small oxer that's x-ed on the front with a little rail behind. That goes about eighteen feet from the cross rail."

This oxer is also low enough to jump at the trot. A horse that is progressing particularly well might be prepared to canter at this point. But keep in mind that a horse is particularly subject to losing confidence early in his jump training.

"I think it's really important not to overface a horse at this point," Cole says. "Never ever put them in a situation where they're frightened."

Also, she points out, never make them work too hard on something that's bound to be physically challenging for them, no matter how hard they worked in their previous careers. "Maybe the first day all I'll do is the pole, the cross rail, to the little oxer. If they've got it, they're happy with it, and they're going straight and relaxed, that's all I want. I'll put them away at that point."

When you have a horse that has been very well trained in another sport, he will probably progress quickly in jumping. It's tempting to work him through the grid quickly so he will be jumping a full course at the canter quickly. Try to resist the temptation.

"Even the most generous of horses can lose confidence quickly," Cole says. "With a horse learning to jump, I train frequently, but just little bits at a time."

In his next lesson, the horse should be asked to repeat the section of the grid that he has already learned. After successfully trotting a number of times, the previously trained horse is probably ready to repeat a short grid at the canter, while the young horse might need a few more lessons before he's ready to keep his balance over obstacles. The cantering grid will have greater distances between obstacles because of the increased length of the stride.

After the horse successfully completes a course of a pole and two jumps, Cole adds a second cross rail beyond the oxer. The pole and the three fences have created a grid that provides safe, easy jumping experiences for the horse.

Perhaps the best thing about the layout is that the horse has been set up for success and confidence building. "There are no options," Cole says. "If he goes forward, he will put in the correct number of strides."

Occasionally, even a willing horse has trouble with the grid. "If he's the kind of horse that can't judge the number of strides, I'll put in a placing pole," Cole says. The pole goes on the ground between fences to force the horse to take a stride over it. This helps him get himself in the correct spot for takeoff; otherwise, his rider will have to cue him and he hasn't learned as much as he should.

The placing pole on the ground means a little extra work for the rider as well as the horse. "You have to ride them a little stronger because there's one more thing to look at," Cole says.

The placing pole can also be used to make wings on the jumps to force the horse to approach straight. Older, experienced horses are very good at finding the easiest way to do something, and easier sometimes means approaching a jump at an angle so they have more room to make the jump.

Cole believes this shouldn't be permitted at this point, even if the horse jumps cleanly. "They start by shifting a little," she says. "Then they move a little more, and then they're run out. You've got to nip that in the bud."

Later on in his jumping career, a horse intended for open competitions where time counts might be trained to jump at an angle at the rider's request. But during his early days of training, he must jump straight.

Jumping a grid provides an excellent foundation for the horse's new career. It gives him experience in jumping, helps him learn when to take off to get over jumps, and gives him good overall exercise. Most important, it gives him confidence, both in his ability to make the jumps and in his ability to make decisions.

"Most horses don't want correction as they go," Cole points out. "If you're clever enough with the exercise, you're not training the horse, the exercise is." Horses, like people, are very fond of thinking that their success is their own doing.

ADVANCING IN JUMPING

Once a horse has mastered jumps in a grid, he's ready for new challenges. To succeed either in competition or in the field, he will have to learn to make decisions on his own.

THE SINGLE FENCE

The option-free grid tells the horse when to take off. It gives him confidence that he can make the right decisions, even though the location

A horse moves on to higher jumps, verticals, and distracting greenery only after he masters his simple grids.

of the obstacles in the grid allows only one decision that will work. In the real world, he really will have to make the decisions. He's going to have to jump fences with no preparatory obstacles that place him exactly in the right spot.

You might try an extremely confident horse with a small cross-rail fence at the canter as soon as he's regularly jumping a grid with few mistakes. If he becomes upset or knocks down the single fence, he needs either more work on the grid or a more careful approach to the single fence.

Set the solitary cross-rail fence at the height it can be trotted. When the horse can trot it successfully and repeatedly, try it at a slow canter. The trotting will have given the horse the confidence that he can handle the obstacle, and that confidence should remain as the horse changes to the canter.

Previously trained horses vary in their levels of confidence. One that was successful and happy in his former career will probably maintain his confidence during his basic jump training, provided he isn't over challenged. A horse carrying unhappy work experiences into jumping may need the most careful approach possible, and that means taking a step backward with more work at grid.

DIFFERENT OBSTACLES

The horse will also need work over a variety of obstacles, either as part of his initial grid or as single fences. Your goal should be for the horse never to lose confidence by failing at a jump, and success is most likely achieved when the next new kind of fence is similar to the previous one. Adult horses are even more likely than young ones to be most comfortable with the familiar.

Follow the cross rail with an oxer composed of a cross rail and a small vertical. Then try the vertical alone. A plain post-and-rail vertical might be followed by a fence that features the familiar rail on top, but a gate underneath. Then add brush under the gate, or return to the plain vertical, followed by a vertical with brush on top. Use the most logical progression possible as you construct jumps.

HIGHER OBSTACLES

Height should also be added gradually, although big, confident, adult horses often progress more quickly to higher fences than younger ones, since they are physically more ready to do it. It's easiest to add height to post-and-rail verticals, but a horse that jumps another kind of fence more enthusiastically may do better if height is added to his favorite fence first.

An adult horse that quickly moves to greater heights may actually move faster than his rider. Nancy Cole points out that it's just as dangerous to overface the rider as the horse.

"A rider's lack of confidence is felt immediately by the horse," she says. "A horse can lose his confidence very quickly if the rider is overfaced."

MOVING OFF THE RAIL

In the show ring or field, all fences are not neatly located on the rail or perimeter. The horse will have to learn to jump fences that require him to approach from unfamiliar directions and different angles. This part of jump training may be easier with previously trained horses than young ones, since their earlier work may have given them experience with performing in various locations within a ring.

The horse should reliably meet and jump obstacles straight, but at some point you'll want to add fences to be jumped at an angle. Also add fences at unexpected spots in the ring. Make sure at first that the angled or unexpected fences are familiar obstacles that the horse knows and jumps well. Remember to add just one new element at a time as you expand the horse's horizons.

New obstacles in different locations will be important to the horse in several ways. Not only will he learn skills he'll need in his later jumping career, he will also be challenged by his training sessions and remain interested in his new work. The older and more experienced the horse, the more likely he is to become bored by familiar routine.

FLYING CHANGE OF LEAD

Having to jump obstacles in different locations and at angles requires the horse to learn to change his lead leg at the canter, since his direction usually changes as he aims for the next fence. All horses learning to jump courses need to learn the flying change, but some adult career changers may have already learned to do it.

Horses that have learned more than a minimal level of dressage, as well as most horses that have performed in Western sports, will probably have been taught the flying change. Many Thoroughbred racehorses will know how to change leads; although some that raced exclusively at six furlongs or less may have never been asked to do it. Beyond that distance, the change is necessary to relieve leg fatigue. There's the rare horse that can run a mile and a quarter without changing leads, but he's usually so valuable that he won't be available for retraining anyway.

Standardbred racehorses won't have a clue about changing leads. They won't even know how to take a lead from the trot at the request of the rider. See Chapters Four and Six for information on leads and former driving horses.

Riding horses that know the flying change have usually learned to do it in one of two ways. They have either been taught to slow to a trot for a stride or two, or—if trained more professionally—to collect slightly before being asked for a new lead with a reversal of the canter aids. Those that slow to a trot are supposed to eventually shorten that trot to nothing but a hesitation, but some never do, and a little trotting stride remains.

Some sports, even those in which the flying change is important, never ask the horse for the change on anything but a turn or curve, which makes it much easier for the horse to accomplish. The horse's instinct is to use the lead on the side of the direction he's moving, so the flying change on a curve comes naturally. Only slight cues are required.

In jumping, it's often enough for the horse to be able to do his flying changes on a curve, so you may not want to train further if the horse can do it at all. But the horse may be able to do more, and it's worthwhile to know about it and to help him maintain the skill.

A horse trained in the higher levels of dressage may have learned to do the flying change on a straight line—a move that's prompted by the same reversal of canter aids. The aids usually have to be more strenuously applied in a straight line change of leads—during early training at least—since the instinct for the correct lead on a turn isn't present to help out.

Thoroughbred racehorses that can do a flying change usually know how to do it on the straightaway, even though they are rarely well trained in other basics. They are usually asked for their change about midway down the homestretch when leg fatigue sets in. The jockey's signal is often minimal. Sometimes the signal is a little boot pressure behind the girth on the opposite side of the new lead, but more often it is just a slight shift of weight to the side of the requested lead.

In a sense, instinct helps here too, even though there's no turn. Leg fatigue encourages some horses to make the change on their own. Whether this full-gallop flying change will easily translate to a change at a more sedate canter depends on the horse, but if the horse could do it at a gallop, you know that he's physically capable of doing it at a canter.

FLEXIBILITY

Horses that are expected to complete a course of jumps in a ring are going to have to be flexible to get from jump to jump in a position to take off reasonably straight. Previously trained horses vary dramatically in how flexible they have become in their first sports.

Horses that have been used for casual riding, trails, racing, or driving will probably not have been asked to do much bending. Dressage horses, Western sport horses, or horses used in mounted games will most likely have become quite flexible.

A horse that needs to be more supple should do plenty of work at the trot in school figures, performed equally in both directions. Large and small circles, figure eights, serpentines—all done while the horse maintains balance and a steady pace—will help him become flexible.

Training for suppleness is helpful in improving the horse's ability to turn, but it's also valuable in improving his actual jumping. Suppling exercises stretch the muscles, which allow the horse to perform over a wider range without strain or injury. A supple horse jumps better than a stiff one, even straight ahead.

BAD HABITS

Previously trained horses are no more likely than green horses to develop bad jumping habits that later have to be corrected. But they do sometimes bring to their new sport habits acquired in their earlier careers.

WATER JUMPS

Few horses like to put their feet in water. It may be that they are afraid of monsters lurking under the surface, or it may be the very sensible worry of exposing their sensitive hooves to unknown footing. Most horses avoid water whenever possible.

This instinct works against successful jumps over water in some horses, while it helps others. Some horses avoid touching the water in an obstacle by leaping clear, while others hesitate and refuse unless forced to jump. Horses are never calm and confident over water jumps.

A horse may have been previously trained out of his instinct not to put his feet in water. A horse used on trails may no longer have any qualms about marching right through standing water.

Such a horse, when asked to go over a water jump, won't worry about putting a foot in the water and may be more careless than other horses. At the least, he won't have much of the instinctive revulsion to water underfoot to help propel himself over it. A former trail horse may need to be trained over water jumps that include one or more rails to encourage him to jump high and wide.

CARELESSNESS

Careless horses can be young or old, previously trained or not. Surprisingly, a very confident, bold horse is sometimes also a careless one. A mature horse, experienced in being asked to perform, may not be as careful as he should be with his hooves, especially if he's smart enough to know that he really isn't going to be hurt much if he touches a pole.

There is no foolproof and completely safe way to make a jumper, experienced or not, more careful over fences. Some trainers advocate poling or rapping techniques in which an assistant, standing alongside the fence, taps the horse's shin or ankle as he reaches the high point of his jump. The assumption is that the horse will jump higher than he thinks he needs to next time in order to avoid the hit.

The problem with using this method with smart and mature horses—apart from the fact that it's illegal in many places—is that the horse soon figures out that the rap only happens when there's a person near the jump. In the show ring or field, he may revert to his sloppy jumps as soon as he sees that nobody is near the obstacle.

Some experienced, adult horses are careless out of boredom, or they become careless if their training program is overly routine. If their training includes the same fences in the same order with the same number and kinds of strides required every time, they may not make enough effort to jump cleanly.

It's dangerous to assume that the horse will suddenly become a meticulous jumper in a show ring or the field when faced with new, interesting jumps presented in a challenging order. His carelessness may have become a habit.

Vary his routine. Use as many different kinds of fences as you can construct. Approach them in a different order, with different combinations and different amounts of cantering and jumping. Variety may solve the problem of carelessness with no further work.

A talented jumper may continue to advance through bigger courses, more difficult obstacles, and jumping rounds that require speed as well as height. Any roadblock he reaches should be approached by going one step back to the previous training level—all the way back to grids if necessary. In fact, as Nancy Cole says, a return to the very basics for a lesson or two can benefit many horses.

"If you're having a problem with a horse, go back to the basics—forward from the leg, straight, and relaxed," she says. "It's the foundation for everything."

CHAPTER TEN

Western Sports

THE WESTERN PERFORMANCE SPORTS CONSTITUTE NORTH America's prime contribution to the world of equestrian activities. The events simulate the work involved in settling the West and operating cattle ranches, and they're enjoyed by riders and spectators for both the athleticism they require and the nostalgia that surrounds them.

The speed sports of barrel racing and pole bending require the speed and agility that a Pony Express rider might have used. The cattle sports—cutting, roping, steer wrestling, and team penning—directly imitate the cowboy's work. Reining showcases the specific movements used in cattle work.

Some ranch horses still do this work, of course, and some of them compete in an occasional show and perform in a few rodeos in their spare time. But most horses that compete in Western performance events are not working ranch horses. Instead, they are riding horses, either show specialists or general use animals. They're mostly members of one of the so-called stock breeds, horses whose ancestors really did the work that Western performance horses now imitate.

But there is room in Western events for horses whose ancestors never set hoof across the Mississippi. You will indeed see far more Quarter Horses, Appaloosas, and Paints in Western sports, but you will see Morgans, Arabs, Thoroughbreds, and others as well. Some breeds are more likely than others to provide the kind of animal needed in the events, and some events are more likely than others to be suitable for non-stock breeds and horses coming out of other sports.

Competition in Western performance sports is offered in several different venues, and the sponsorship of the particular event helps determine whether retrained horses of non-stock breeds can compete. But there are so many different shows under such a wide variety of sponsors that every horse is a potential competitor.

Breed organizations are the most restrictive. The American Quarter Horse Association, whose shows may offer almost all the Western events, are open only to registered Quarter Horses. Paint, Appaloosa, Palomino, Buckskin, and other registries do the same thing.

An all-breeds horse show might offer some of the Western events, and these will include classes open to horses of any breed. A large all-breeds show may also include classes open only to horses of specific breeds, but there should be equivalent unrestricted classes offered too.

Some of the events appear in rodeos. Calf roping and steer wrestling are part of most rodeos, and barrel racing is included in many. There are sanctioned and nonsanctioned rodeos, professional, amateur, and open rodeos, rodeos for children, prisoners, women, Native Americans, and others. There's a rodeo for almost every horse and rider.

Shows sanctioned by the governing bodies of the individual sports offer plenty of classes and categories. At the highest levels of the specialty shows, the performance standards are probably beyond the reach of most retrained horses. But there is competition at the novice as well as the championship level, and everything in between. Most of these sport organizations have no restrictions on the breed and background of the horses, although there are age and experience categories that limit entry into particular events.

What all this means is that there is plenty of opportunity for a rider to choose a horse with a sport in mind, train him for it, and enter him into competition. The variety of venues also gives those riders who are thinking about retraining a particular horse the opportunity to judge the sport before training actually begins.

The reality doesn't always coincide with the image. Sid Bresnan, who trains and competes with roping horses, says events like roping are not for all horses and riders.

"Go see the events," he says. "Make sure it's really something you want to do. It's more physical than a lot of people think. It's hard on horse and rider, and not everybody is capable of doing it."

Both novice competitors and more experienced people can benefit by traveling to as many shows as possible to see what a successful horse looks like. Many dramatically different physical characteristics are seen in very good horses in Western sports. In most of the sports, you'll see good horses with conformation characteristics that an equally good horse in other equine activities is unlikely to have. Some of these characteristics are outright flaws in other sports.

Form definitely follows function in the Western sports. If the horse can do the job, it doesn't matter what he looks like. There is little subjective judgment in deciding who wins. The events are demanding, sometimes rough, and often dangerous to horse and rider.

Good looks count for very little. What does count is utility, as you'll see when we consider the conformation and personality characteristics to look for in a horse that you might want to train for a Western performance sport.

CONFORMATION REQUIREMENTS

The Western events vary in their demands on the horse, but there are a few general characteristics that are important in all of them. First comes overall sturdiness. More than any other equine activity, the Western performance sports demand horses that can stand up under physical stress. The stress differs in some of the sports, but each event is physically demanding.

The horses need strong frames, heavy bone in the lower leg, and bodies that are wide rather than narrow. Within the individual sports, there are different interpretations of what sturdiness means, but all the events require some variation of it.

They also all require quickness. In the case of the Western sports, quickness doesn't mean speed. Quickness is speed plus agility, and it gives the horse the ability to call on his speed immediately, from full

*This cutting mare has the sturdy build, the quickness, and the moderate
size that makes her ideal for most Western sports.*

gallop or from a stop, from one direction to another. The start-and-stop
sports need quickness to keep up with calves or steers, while the speed
sports need quickness to change direction without losing time.

Western performance horses also must be of no more than moderate height, but they can't be correspondingly light in weight. This is a
function of the need for sturdiness and agility. A tall horse is rarely
agile, and a light horse is rarely sturdy.

Those are the general guidelines—sturdy, quick, and not too tall.
Many breeds can provide candidates that fit them. But individual sports
have their own additional requirements.

THE SPEED SPORTS

Barrel racing is the most popular of the Western speed sports. It's offered in more and more venues, and the prize money is substantial. But there are other speed events, all featuring short courses with horses running against the clock rather than each other. In pole bending, the horses weave a serpentine path through a series of poles. In stake races, the horses complete half the barrel race's cloverleaf. In flag races and similar racing games, the rider plucks an object out of, or places one into, a barrel or other marker.

What all the events have in common is the kind of horse that excels. More than any other Western performance sport, the speed events—barrel racing in particular—favor non-stock breeds and horses coming out of other sports.

The horses still have to be quick and agile in order to get themselves around barrels or poles, but a speed event includes enough pure galloping that a bigger, long-striding horse can often beat a quick, shorter one. The very best speed performers are usually stock horses with Thoroughbred blood for the extra stride length and more raw speed.

The American Quarter Horse Association permits the registration of part-Thoroughbred animals, and as generations go by, more and more Thoroughbred blood is being bred into Quarter Horses intended for racing. On the racetrack, many top performers are now seven-eighths and fifteen-sixteenths Thoroughbred. These bloodlines are also appearing in the speed events in shows and rodeos.

So a Thoroughbred or a mostly Thoroughbred warmblood would not be out of place in Western speed events these days. He would be eligible to compete in all but breed shows.

But not all are the right physical type. The modern barrel horse is taller than other Western performers, but not very tall by Thoroughbred or warmblood standards. Preferences among riders vary, but most experienced performers want a horse of about 15.2 hands, give or take an inch or so. Taller horses usually can't get their bodies around obstacles quickly enough, and shorter ones lack the stride length to put up good times.

Speed horses need average size and agility to get themselves around the obstacles quickly and safely.

This height requirement, although more favorable to horses of non-stock breeds than the other sports, does eliminate the taller Thoroughbreds and part-Thoroughbreds. A taller horse could certainly hope to compete at lower levels, and some tall horses may be so agile that they can manage the turns, but most good non-stock candidates will come from smaller Thoroughbreds and crosses.

The ideal height limits some Arabs, too. Many of them, otherwise good candidates for barrels, are too short for the kind of straightaway speed needed to excel.

Flexibility is important in the speed events, so horses with necks a little longer and thinner than desirable in a stock horse sometimes do very well. They are able to wrap themselves around the obstacles without losing as much ground as a short-necked horse might. A back slightly longer than ideal also helps in flexibility. Again, horses of Thoroughbred type often have longer necks and backs than stock horses.

Thoroughbreds also have the long and sloping shoulder that gives good stride length on the straightaway. Many stock breeds have shorter and straighter shoulders, so Thoroughbred blood—whether pure or part of a cross—is valuable for the shape of shoulder it often contributes.

What Thoroughbreds often don't have is the short pastern that's important to soundness in a speed horse. The tight turns and bursts of speed are extremely stressful on the feet and legs, and long, sloping pasterns often can't survive. Some speed horses have pasterns much more upright than you see on horses in other sports, but their short length allows them to take more stress without giving way.

A good barrel horse certainly needs the typical wide hindquarters in order to slow down, turn, then accelerate around a barrel or end pole. Traditional Thoroughbreds have narrow hindquarters, but some bred for modern racing are broad in the rear. Since most flat races in North America are now run at six furlongs or less, horses that can accelerate

Speed-sport horses are broad in the hindquarters like stock horses, but they tend to be a little taller and have longer strides.

over short distances have been bred in huge numbers over the past several decades.

Warmbloods often have wide hindquarters, depending on how much draft blood the particular breed includes. Unfortunately, the warmbloods with enough draft ancestry to have good, wide hindquarters probably don't have enough speed to compete in barrel racing or other speed events. Arabs may or may not be wide behind, depending on whether their parents were bred for looks or work.

Standardbreds are a possibility, but you'll need to look for trotters rather than pacers. It's not the gait that's the problem. As you saw in Chapter Six, most pacers can be converted to the trot. But pacers are almost always far too narrow in the hindquarters to produce the start-and-stop power needed in barrel racing. Trotters are usually wide enough, although you never know just how well they can gallop until you try them.

CATTLE SPORTS

Four important Western performance events involve cattle. Each of them calls for a horse whose instincts are nearly as important as his physical qualities.

The successful cattle-sport horse has to understand steers or calves well enough to follow their moves almost without thinking. The best cow horses understand so well that they seem to be able to predict the moves of individual cattle. Cow sense is probably inherited; although there are many offspring of good cow horses that are afraid of calves, and plenty of horses whose parents never saw a steer, that can handle them perfectly.

A horse bred for cattle work has probably been used or at least tried in one of the sports, but it's possible to find a horse with cow sense in another unrelated sport. Possible, but not easy.

It's difficult to predict which horse might have it and which doesn't without trying them out with cattle. If you have access to cattle, try riding the prospect among them. First, make sure that he's not afraid of them. Then, see if he's curious about the animals, interested in following them, and willing to be told to track them.

Lacking cattle, try other small animals. Cow horses often show similar curiosity with chickens, dogs, and other little creatures. Individual horses of any breed can have this kind of curiosity. Many like to chase and play with animals of other species. Some are quite aggressive with these animals, and that's not something that you want to see. Enough aggression to be willing to separate a herd-bound animal or chase one in a playful manner is just fine, but a horse that wants to injure the animal might be too aggressive for sport.

Surprisingly, pony breeds used mostly for English riding often work very well with small animals. You might not call it cow sense when a Shetland or Connemara chases a dog, but it does show the right kind of mind-set. A crossbred horse with one of these breeds in his background might have what the cattle sports need.

A horse with little interest in any of the animals might be trainable for some of the sports, including roping and steer wrestling. He's unlikely to do well in cutting or team penning. A horse that's afraid of small animals is not a good prospect for any of the cattle sports.

Like all Western performance horses, a cow horse needs to be quick. He has to be able to track the unpredictable and sudden movement of calves and steers. He has to have a particularly good rear end, since the cattle will force him to make sudden stops and to accelerate instantly. But beyond the hindquarters and the cow sense, the individual cattle sports have their own physical requirements.

CUTTING

The cutting horse needs a low natural head carriage, a characteristic that Thoroughbreds, Thoroughbred crosses, and Standardbreds often share with stock horses. Arabs and Morgans usually don't.

Training can lower the head somewhat, but a horse whose neck is set onto his shoulders in a manner that forces him to carry his head high will never be able to drop his neck enough to bring him eye-to-eye with a calf. It's an absolute requirement of cutting.

In addition, the head, neck, and shoulders of a cutting horse have to be comparatively light. A horse that's heavy in front is unable to shift his front end to track the back and forth movements of a calf trying to find a way to return to his herd. There's a little flexibility in this requirement. A neck that's a little long but slender will work, as will one that's shorter but not too thick.

ROPING

In roping, the horse needs plenty of body weight to counteract the weight of the steer or calf. This calls for a special body type.

"I like a horse with a thick shoulder, a short neck, a short back, as well as the big hind end," Sid Bresnan says. "You want something that's short and strong that can pull and stop on his hind end."

The shoulder is particularly important in roping, since the rider's end of the rope is attached to the horn. The shoulder takes the brunt of

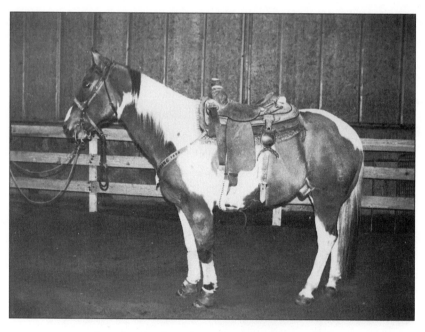

A good roping horse has to be sturdy, short-necked, and very strong in the shoulder.

the pull. Extremely low withers make it almost impossible to keep a saddle in place under the stress of roping, so you need to look for some definition there.

In modern rodeos and show sports, there are two kinds of roping: calf roping and team roping. The two versions have slightly different demands on the horses that perform in them, so a wide range of animals can qualify for at least one aspect of roping.

Calf roping is the most demanding for man and horse because of the extreme speed and the stress on the body that it brings. In addition to making sure the calf roping prospect has a short, thick body, Sid Bresnan advises taking a good look at the feet.

"You need a really good hoof all around," he says. "If you have trouble keeping a wall on the hoof just trail riding, it's not going to be easy. You'll need a really good blacksmith."

In sports like jumping, good feet in front are more important than behind, while in others the reverse is true. In roping, you need both. Horses with pony blood often have the kind of hard, sturdy feet needed in a roping horse, and they usually have the right body shape—short and thick. They probably don't have the weight or quickness, unless size and speed have been crossbred into them. But a crossbred pony is definitely worth a look.

Other riding breeds rarely have the body shape and quickness combined in such a way to make them calf-roping prospects. Arabs and Thoroughbreds are usually not thick enough, lacking the necessary bone substance, while draft-type horses aren't quick enough.

Two horses are used in team roping, and one of the jobs is much less demanding than the other. The heeler catches up with the steer, putting his rider in a position to rope the hind legs of the animal. The heading horse carries his rider to the point where he can rope the horns. The horses must maintain a pull on the rope to control the steer's movement. Both jobs require skill, but heading has more physical demands than heeling.

"You can make any horse a heeling horse," Bresnan says. "He just has to run to the hole and stop. A heading horse has to be very strong in the shoulder, because once you rope the horns you're pulling hundreds of pounds of steer to the right. A fine-boned animal is not going to be able to pull well enough."

This eliminates many riding horses as header prospects. As with calf roping, most draft-type horses don't have the speed to reach the steer. Standardbreds tend to have slightly heavier bone than light riding horses, and sometimes they have very strong shoulders. If they have speed at the gallop, they might be tried.

Most light riding horses do have the physical qualifications to be heeling horses. They need some quickness to break out of the box and some speed to reach the steer. They need good bone and conformation from the hock down, because they do have to stop suddenly. Thoroughbreds can heel, as can Arabs, fast Morgans, trotting Standardbreds, and crosses of most of these breeds.

TEAM PENNING

Of all the cattle sports, team penning is most suitable for non-stock horses and animals coming out of different sports. A team-penning horse can be a little lighter than a roping horse, a little higher headed than a cutting horse, and a little shorter and not quite as fast on the straightaway as a barrel horse.

The horse does need many of the same qualities as horses in the other events. The penning horse has to gallop across an arena like a barrel horse, change direction with his front end like a cutting horse, and score cattle like a roping horse. But because he has to do each of these jobs, he can be less than perfectly conformed for any one of them and still excel. So, horses of different breeds and backgrounds may have a better chance to compete successfully in team penning than in any other Western performance event.

If there's one word to describe the ideal team penning horse, it's average. He shouldn't be too tall or too short, because he needs stride length for the straight runs and he needs agility for tight, sudden turns. Horses of 15.1 to 15.2 hands are ideal, but animals both shorter and taller also perform well. Thoroughbreds and warmbloods are often taller than this, and Arabs and Morgans are often shorter, but each of these breeds has plenty of members that qualify. Most Standardbreds are exactly right in terms of height.

The team-penning horse needs the wide hindquarters of the typical Western performance horse, but the presence of two teammates means that his turns and stops don't always have to be quite as sudden as those in other sports. He doesn't need a particularly strong shoulder, and his neck can be a little too short or a little too long without compromising his performance. The same is true of backs.

STEER WRESTLING

In the final cattle sport, steer wrestling or bulldogging, average won't do. Horses of any background can be used, but they have to fit within a specific and narrow pattern. They have to be very short so that the rider has to make only a short drop from horse to steer. They have to be very quick, because they have to be able to reach a steer within seconds and keep right next to it. They have to be sturdy and sound to take the pounding that comes with repeated dashes across arenas.

Few horses other than members of stock breeds are likely to have these qualifications. The combination of extreme speed, shortness, and sturdiness is rare except in horses of traditional Quarter Horse breeding. But an occasional pony-Thoroughbred cross might have the right combination of characteristics. A few minutes spent ringside in a pony hunter class at an English show might show you a few prospects. Their owners would probably be horrified that somebody was even considering the possibility of using their ponies as steer-wrestling horses, but some of the ponies might be very good at it.

REINING

Reining is the Western equivalent of dressage, and horses intended for reining competition need many of the same qualities as their English counterparts. But since they're judged subjectively, their physical characteristics have to be enclosed in a Western-style package.

Reining horses have to look like stock horses to compete success-fully, but horses of other breeds and backgrounds can and do perform well in competition. It's true that reining classes are held in breed shows, but a brief reining test is a common part of all-breed Western horse classes too. There also are shows and extensive show circuits devoted exclusively to reining horses. As with dressage, many of the reining movements provide a useful foundation for any working Western horse. So, reining instruction will be useful for almost any horse you choose to bring to it.

Some horses have an easier time than others with the movements of reining. If you wish to compete, or even train extensively in reining, you should look for a horse that is conformed for the work.

Reining movements are stylized versions of the movements made by working cow horses, so they are supposed to be performed with the headset and body shape that a horse needs to handle cattle. That means a low head and neck, one set as near as possible to a right angle to his shoulder. During some of the moves, he will be expected to carry his head even lower than that. A naturally high head won't work in reining any more than in cutting.

The square stop is an important movement itself, but it's also the foundation for other reining movements, like the spin, the rollback, and the rein back. It's not enough to stop just by ceasing forward move-ment. A reining horse has to stop with his hindquarters well under-neath, so the prospect must have the kind of rear end that permits the hocks to be brought under his belly as he stops.

His shoulders will have to come up at the same time, so his with-ers can't be unusually high. A croup-high horse or one whose croup is level with his withers, but can still bring his hocks underneath, can do this kind of stop. High withers will eliminate many horses of non-stock breeds from being true reining prospects.

Height is not important, although a very tall horse rarely has the agility to do the high-speed turns and pivots required by the sport. The front end should be fairly light to allow the pivots, even though train-ing in collection will teach the horse to lighten his own front end by moving his center of balance back.

You will find horses in most of the riding and light driving breeds that have the physical characteristics needed for reining. To succeed in competition, you have to make sure that the horse has a stock-type appearance. Judges aren't supposed to rate anything but performance, but many do.

As horse generations go by, the stock appearance will become less necessary, since so much Thoroughbred blood now appears in registered Quarter Horses and other stock breeds. In the meantime, look for compact rather than rangy, short-to-medium rather than tall, and muscular rather than smooth.

EQUIPMENT

The equipment used in the individual events varies according to the traditions of the sport, the rules of the sponsoring organization, and years of experience by riders and trainers. As in any sport, there are both traditionalists and innovators, and you will find plenty of choices in and among the sports.

It's fortunate that there are so many possible choices. Horses new to challenging sports need special care in the selection and fitting of tack.

BRIDLE AND BIT

Your first choice will be between a browband and a sliding-ear or a fixed, single-ear headstall. It probably won't matter much to the horse, although an animal coming out of the English sports will have invariably used a browband. There's a slight possibility that the single-ear headstall may cause a little irritation around the ear at first, but this should disappear as soon as his skin becomes accustomed to the rubbing. To avoid irritation altogether, choose a browband. It's acceptable in all sports today.

Old-time Western horsemen preferred the single-ear headstall to the browband style, feeling that it showed off a beautiful stock-horse head. In the performance sports, a beautiful head doesn't win any points. Pick whichever bridle you prefer, unless you're afraid that your horse looks too Thoroughbred or may look otherwise too "unacceptable" and that judges might find him more acceptable without the browband.

You will have more than two choices when you pick a bit. Some show rules require the use of a curb bit on any adult Western horse. If you intend to compete in classes at these shows, your horse will have to learn to use a curb. See Chapter Five for information on the conversion from snaffle to curb.

In other events, you have the option of using a curb, snaffle, or other bit. Many competitors train and race in plain O- or D-ring snaffles, the mildest bits possible. Others go a step closer to the curb, choosing a shanked snaffle for both training and competition. It's comfortable, like a snaffle, but it provides the leverage sometimes needed for the abrupt stops and turns.

"I like to stay off a horse's mouth," Sid Bresnan says. "I start all horses in a plain snaffle to see how they go with no shank. But most respond best with a snaffle with a five-inch shank. Once in a while, I'll switch to a stronger bit, but you want them to respond to a shift in your weight, not so much to the bit."

Some riders in each of the sports choose more severe bits. But even with an unjointed curb, the modern tendency is to use a mild one with a low port and relatively short shanks. Reiners, traditionally users of extremely long shanks, now often use shanks shorter than the eight-and-a-half inches allowed. What is lost in leverage is made up for in comfort for the horse.

If the longer shanks are indeed going to be used, take time and care in introducing the bit to the previously trained horse, especially one that was trained English style. He may never have used a curb at all; if he did, it was probably part of a double bridle and not his primary controlling bit. Unless he was a Tennessee Walking Horse, he will never have felt anything like the leverage of an eight-inch shank.

During the initial days of any training or retraining project, fear of equipment is the last thing you want to instill. A sudden and unexpected tightening of a curb strap, a heavy pull on the poll, or a rap against the roof of the mouth can cause a horse to associate pain with his new sport. First impressions are most remembered, and pain is an impression he and you can do without.

Whichever kind of bit you choose, consider its weight. Horses coming out of English sports and casual riding are usually accustomed to lightweight bits. The ordinary Western curb will be heavier than expected. The horse can be introduced gradually to the heavier bit, but most horses will make the transition to the new style of bit more quickly and comfortably if they are not expected to become accustomed to a heavier weight at the same time.

Look for a lightweight curb or shanked snaffle for the transition period. A horse destined for a sport where free head movement is necessary—cutting, penning, and the speed sports—might be best kept in a light bit, even a hollow-mouthed aluminum one, forever.

SADDLES

The choice of saddle is governed largely by the sport that you intend to pursue with your retrained horse. Speed sports call for a flat saddle and stirrup bars brought slightly forward to allow the rider to sit forward at the gallop. Reiners prefer a built-up front to give them a deeper seat and a center of balance transferred further back. Ropers need a heavy-duty horn.

Each kind of saddle will require a period of transition for a horse coming out of another sport, even another Western one. Changes in the center of balance as well as the location of cinches and flaps can cause pain in a horse that is unaccustomed to weight and pressure in particular locations.

In the case of a horse coming out of an English sport, the period of transition may have to be longer. Consult Chapter Five for information on converting him to carrying the larger and heavier Western saddle.

The athletic nature of the Western sports means that saddle fitting is especially important with the horse new to the sport. The basic rules of fitting and padding are those discussed in Chapter Five, but there are additional points to consider.

The sudden stops, starts, and turns of the Western performance sports mean much greater potential for injury caused by saddles than you'll find in trail or pleasure riding. Good fitting is a must, and sometimes that means a custom saddle. A saddle that almost fits won't stay in place under the pressure of turns. A slipped saddle is dangerous for the rider and usually painful for the horse.

Even saddles that fit perfectly need at least one blanket underneath for cushioning. The blanket is usually wool or part wool, for absorbency and padding.

Many performance riders now use specially designed saddle pads under or instead of the traditional blankets. These can range from $30, shaped, synthetic-fleece pads with a half-inch of soft filling to a $150 pad with gel inserts. What they have in common is a design that helps prevent trauma to the back and shoulders.

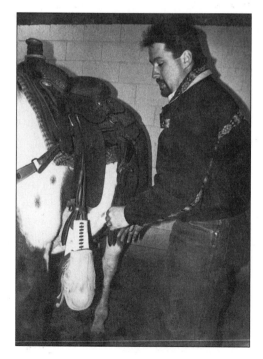

Horses new to Western sports have to become accustomed to the flank cinch.

In roping, extra care must be taken to prevent the shoulders from being injured from the jerk of the roped steer or calf.

"Use the proper equipment," Sid Bresnan says. "You need really good cushioning for the shoulders. Once the shoulders are sore, the horse doesn't want to work."

The flank cinch is needed in several of the sports, and its use is not optional, even with a horse that doesn't like it.

"It controls where your saddle sits," Sid Bresnan says. "When you rope, the 200 pounds of calf pulls away on the front of the saddle. The rear cinch holds the back of the saddle down so the front doesn't ride on the shoulder."

The rear cinch must be introduced gradually to a horse that has never worn one. Use it with a spacer to make sure that it doesn't slip too far back onto the sensitive flesh of the flanks, and tighten it slowly over a period of days or weeks. Leave it even looser than normal if you have a horse that seems to resent its presence.

Since flank cinches are normally leather, the material may bother some horses trained originally in other sports—even Western activities. Good-quality leather girths are used on dressage and jumping horses, but most casual riding, both English and Western, is done with web or string girths. Leather straps can irritate some equine skin, so keep an eye on the area under the flank cinch as the horse becomes used to it.

OTHER EQUIPMENT

Tie-downs are almost always used in roping and the speed sports, and sometimes in team penning. In other sports, they are either prohibited or frowned upon.

The tie-down keeps the horse from throwing up his head and serves the same function as the standing martingale in English use. In Western use, it's attached to a separate cable or flat noseband that isn't buckled directly under the chin. It puts a different kind of pressure on the nose, but a horse used to a standing martingale will probably adjust to the confinement of the tie-down.

What will be a little more difficult for him will be the nature of the pressure on the nose. The pressure is more direct, since little of it is absorbed by the headstall, and the horse's nose may get sore while he's learning to keep his head down and his nose in. You may have to adjust the spot where the noseband lies on the nose to avoid soreness.

Most Western performance horses are trained in bandages, boots, or both, and many compete with various items of protective equipment. The choice depends on the sport, the horse's stride, and the level at which you are training or competing.

Horses expected to do lateral moves usually need some protection on the lower legs and ankles because of the danger of one hoof striking another leg. Horses expected to do more than the occasional sliding stop might need skid boots to protect the back of the fetlock. Barrel racers and reiners often need splint boots to protect the inside of the front fetlock.

During the early days of training, the horse is unlikely to be asked for the kind of effort that produces injury. On the other hand, his body is probably not used to irritation in particular areas, and he's especially vulnerable to cuts and scrapes that wouldn't break the skin later in training.

The goal during the first part of retraining is to use enough protective equipment to prevent injury and unpleasant experiences, but not so much that he has more to get used to than is necessary. This may mean regular reassessment of his need for bandages, boots, and wraps, perhaps by asking a friend to watch him for overreaching or brushing as you ride him.

TRAINING FOR THE WESTERN SPORTS

It's beyond the scope of this book to tell you how to train a horse for each of the Western performance sports. If you don't already know something about training, take some lessons or ask for the help of an experienced friend. What we can do here is take a look at some of the aspects of training that differ when you bring a previously trained adult horse into a new Western sport. Most of the points are true of all of the sports, although some are exclusive to individual events.

CONDITIONING

The physical demands of the Western sports are different from other equine activities. More than any other except perhaps polo, they call for horses in excellent physical condition.

Sid Bresnan believes in taking plenty of time getting ready before beginning work in the new sport. Even though he's discussing roping here, his suggestions are valid for any of the demanding events.

"Put sixty minutes of riding on him every day," he says. "You have to get him really fit. Every horse that comes into my barn I work every day, an hour a day. With a fit, athletic horse, the transition is going to be much easier."

Most horses in other sports, even demanding ones, don't work nearly this much. Thoroughbred racehorses in training are asked for a full gallop for only a few minutes a couple of times a week, although they might jog for twenty minutes every day. Standardbreds are more fit, going out every day for several miles of work at speed, but they are never asked for a gallop. Hunters and jumpers rarely work more than every other day, and they usually train for less than an hour.

Obviously, the workload has to be increased gradually. Any horse should be able to stay out for an hour a day, but few are in good enough condition to perform at any kind of speed for that long until they have been in serious training for weeks.

During the conditioning period, the horse can also learn to do the kind of things he'll need later on. If he's coming out of Western pleasure, Western or English trail riding, driving, dressage, or any of several other activities, he's probably never been asked to gallop. After he has developed some conditioning, he can learn to reach the kind of speed he'll need for some of the sports.

He should also learn the contrasting skill that a performance horse needs—the ability to stand still and wait. Many horses from other sports have never had to do this for more than a second or two at a time. But the performance horse has to be able to rouse himself instantly from waiting to action, so he will need practice at standing still but alert.

Many Thoroughbred racehorses learn this skill in the starting gate, but Standardbreds generally don't. They make full-speed starts. Horses used in the English hunter sports rarely wait long before they perform. When they begin to move, it's usually at the walk, then trot, then canter. These horses usually need the most work at alert waiting.

NECK REINING

All the performance sports require a horse to know how to neck rein. It's usually not difficult to teach an English-trained horse to respond to the neck rein, and Chapter Five shows you one easy way to do it.

Once they have learned to neck rein, these horses may have an advantage over Western horses that weren't trained with a snaffle as young animals. The direct rein is occasionally useful in most events, and a horse that knows both neck reining and direct reining can perform movements that the horse that knows only one cannot.

THE STOP

Each of the Western performance sports requires a good stop. In steer wrestling and barrel racing, the horse only has to stop well enough to avoid running into a wall, but sometimes that has to be a very abrupt stop indeed. In the other sports, the stop is a major part of the quality of the performance.

No other equine sport calls for precisely the same kind of stop, but some previously trained horses may have learned to come to a halt from the gallop. Polo ponies know how to do it, although their stop is invariably the first step of a rollback or pivot rather than a movement valued for itself. Driving horses usually know how to do a strong, square stop, but they never do it from the gallop. Most other horses have learned to stop by slowing through the other gaits first, and the sliding stop prized by Western riders will be foreign to them.

Also foreign will be the cues to stop. Horses trained in the English sports, usually with a snaffle, respond first to a pull back on the reins as their cue to stop. Those that were trained with a cue to collect as they halt will also respond to a slight squeeze on or behind the girth.

Both the time constraints and the bits used in the Western sports make the pull back unsuitable. Instead, the rider increases contact while lifting the reins to a higher level than that used in English riding. For a sliding stop, the leg cues are even stronger and applied a little further forward. Chapters Four and Five include information on the differences between the Western and English stops.

A previously trained horse learning the new cues should be converted gradually. Don't try for an abrupt stop from the gallop before the horse learns the new cues from a walk, jog, and slow lope. He must understand and respond to the lifted reins, because they will tell him to lift up his forequarters as he brings his hindquarters underneath him. He must learn not to expect a strong pull back on the reins.

Using "Whoa" or a similar word during the transition lessons will help reinforce his new cues to the stop.

Sometimes, horses resist stopping completely. Unless they come to a complete halt, they will never be in a position to do a sliding stop. They may have been permitted or even encouraged to do a semi-stop in their previous working lives. In most other sports, you come to a complete halt only when you are finished working.

Horses that don't stop completely aren't cured by a heavy pull back on the reins, especially since that serves to reinforce the incorrect stop cues. Try stopping the horse as much as possible on the proper cues, including "Whoa" or another verbal signal, then pull him to one side or another. End all leg aids so that he isn't encouraged to go forward. This exercise may help him associate "Whoa" and the stopping cues with the idea that forward movement ends when he hears and feels them. Don't repeat the exercise too many times, or you may develop a horse with a crooked stop.

Some trainers reinforce the idea of the complete stop by asking the horse to change directions right after stopping. This is a rollback, a more advanced movement, but it can be used in a simple form in training to make the horse realize that a cue to stop means a complete stop. He can't change direction unless he has stopped his forward movement in the first direction.

This exercise also helps a horse understand that the best way to stop, to put himself in a position to change directions and restart, is to move his center of balance back. If his rear feet are underneath him and his forequarters are up, he can make the change of direction far more easily.

DISTRACTIONS

The Western sports include distractions that aren't present in other horse events, and every new participant needs to get used to them. The

The roping horse should learn about the rope before he's expected to carry his rider at the gallop with the rope flying.

Horses in the cattle sports should be permitted to become comfortable around calves and steers.

competition venues tend to be noisier than other kinds of horse shows, since they include bells, timers, loud announcers, livestock, and other distracting sounds.

"Take a new horse to the events," Sid Bresnan advises. "Put him near the fence. Let him hear the speakers and see what's going on."

The individual sports have their own distractions. A new barrel horse should be allowed a close look at barrels, a chance to smell and nuzzle them, a leisurely walk around them, and the sight of them tipping over before he's asked to gallop anywhere near them. A roping horse should have a rope swung over his head, touch his body, and fall on the ground beside him while he's standing comfortably in familiar surroundings.

All potential participants in cattle events need plenty of time around calves or steers, both from the ground and while mounted. If they are afraid of cattle they probably won't be considered for training anyway, but even fearless horses need to learn not to be distracted by the smells, movements, and sounds of livestock.

In timed events, horses should be familiarized with the boxes or chutes that they are going to have to wait in. They should know how to walk in quietly, stand still, and be alert when exiting, even before they begin serious training in breaking out of the box for their events.

PART FIVE

Special Cases

CHAPTER ELEVEN

The Unbroken Adult Horse

TRAINERS VEHEMENTLY DISAGREE ABOUT THE PROPER age to break a horse. Trainers of Standardbreds will have their horses pulling a light training cart in August or September of their yearling year. Trainers of racing Quarter Horses or Thoroughbreds are a little more conservative. They might wait until October to put a rider aboard the yearling.

Trainers in other sports find this to be unreasonably early, and their horses won't be ridden for the first time until the age of two or three. But no matter how conservative, not a single one will tell you that you should wait until the horse is nine or ten years old.

It does happen, however, that some domestic horses manage to get through their youth without being trained. Strictly speaking, the lack of use has been a kind of training in itself. The horse has learned that he can live comfortably, eat well, be sheltered, and be treated affectionately without having to work. He has effectively been trained to be idle.

Training a fully adult horse that has learned these happy lessons is a difficult, time-consuming, and occasionally dangerous task. Just how hard and long the job will take depends upon why the horse is unbroken in the first place.

HOW DID IT HAPPEN?

Sometimes, a horse isn't broken young because of circumstances. An owner might have too many horses and too little time, no facilities in which to train, or no ability to train. He doesn't want or can't afford a professional trainer, and he doesn't want to sell the horse. The years manage to sneak by, and the owner finds himself with an unbroken ten-year-old. A well-cared-for horse in this situation is probably trainable, given time and effort.

A horse injured while young might not have been trained because of his physical condition. If he's now healthy, he can begin training. But any physical problem bad enough to keep him out of training in the past will always have to be considered in the present. A horse in this situation needs a thorough check by a vet who knows the horse's history and your intentions for him.

Some horses remain unbroken as adults because somebody once tried to break them and then gave up. If the original trainer quit because of lack of time or energy, the horse is basically the same as those in the first group—simple circumstances prevented him from being broken at the ideal age.

But if the trainer gave up because the horse did something to frighten him, breaking now may be extremely difficult. Trainer Janet Keffer-Nelson says that this is often the situation with a horse that managed to grow up without being broken.

"If the person who initiated his training got scared and stopped," she says, "the horse will remember that he was left alone after that happened."

Horses may not have great intellects, but they do have excellent memories. A horse that learned, even years ago, that a particular bad behavior means no more work will remember, and probably repeat that bad behavior.

If you are the original owner, you will know why the horse wasn't broken. If you aren't, try to find out who had the horse at the normal breaking age of two or three. You will find it useful to discover the reason for the horse's lack of training.

ADVANTAGES

There aren't many good things to be said about very late breaking, but there are a few. Horses not used by humans until relatively late in their lives are usually sound. Their feet are often especially healthy.

"The foot has had a chance to expand and really hit the ground," Keffer-Nelson says. "The unshod foot is usually very sound." The absence of nails means the absence of nail injuries to the soft tissue of the foot, as well as the absence of hoof-wall damage.

The horse will probably also be sounder in the legs and skeleton than a horse of similar age that's been under saddle or harness for several years. "Their bones and joints have reached full development," Keffer-Nelson says. "They've had a chance to grow and fully develop without stress. Their topline is also strong and ready for work."

INSTINCTS

Instincts are important to all horses, but with older, unbroken ones, instincts can rule. The most important of the instincts is the belief that other horses—the herd—comprise the vital center of life.

"I find that they tend to put their trust in other horses rather than people," Keffer-Nelson says. "They are more distracted by other horses in the ring and by horses in nearby pastures."

Not having had to listen to people, they have learned to listen to other horses. The tendency, easily overcome in young horses, is firmly entrenched in older ones. Whenever possible, try to work the unbroken older horse alone, away from other horses.

The herding instinct can be exploited in young horses, helping to teach them to lead by following another horse, helping them learn to be comfortable on a trail. With an older horse, the tendency to pay attention to other horses rather than the trainer may be so great that it's best to avoid other animals until the trainee changes his allegiance.

Jhaelan, a ten-year-old Morgan-Trakhener cross, remained untrained because of family and work demands. He's a good-natured, intelligent horse capable of doing the dressage work originally envisioned for him. But Keffer-Nelson says he is far too easily distracted in his duties.

"If the horses in the next field say hello, his concentration is gone," she says. "His attention is on them."

The accompanying factor to being overly concerned with other horses is not caring enough about people, trainers included. Older untrained horses rarely feel the need to please human beings, as many young horses do.

"Long lack of use means that they often lack a relationship with humans," Keffer-Nelson says. "The horse has become more self-centered and more self-sufficient. They believe they haven't had to count on people except for food, and that they seem to take for granted."

The strength and unchecked development of the herding instinct means that the trainer is going to have to make an effort to establish his position in the horse's concept of herd. The trainer must be higher in the pecking order in order to gain respect.

This is done relatively easily with a young horse that is invariably low in the pecking order. It's far more difficult with the older horse, whose position has been won and held.

"Be careful to avoid submissive gestures," Keffer-Nelson says. "You might want to put your head underneath the horse's head as you hug him. But a lower-order horse does this. Don't kiss him on the nose. That's a baby-horse gesture."

OVERCOMING HABITS

The unbroken adult horse hasn't acquired the nasty habits that some demonstrate while being ridden, but he may have established a healthy repertoire of field and stable vices. They will probably be slightly different vices from those exhibited by trained horses, and they may be harder to break. The unbroken horse is not used to giving in to human wishes.

THE HARD TO CATCH HORSE

You might think that a horse would be hard to catch only if he expects to have to work every time he's caught and haltered—that an unbroken, unused horse wouldn't be expecting to work and therefore shouldn't mind being caught.

Unfortunately, it doesn't work that way with most horses, and unbroken, older animals are often the most difficult of all to catch in a pasture or corral. Keeping them stalled is no solution, because they need exercise more than ever, both before and during a training program.

Most horses, even unbroken ones, can be lured with grain in a bucket. Some people don't mind bringing grain every time they want the horse, and never bother to train him out of the habit; others would rather not have to remember a bribe every time.

Lure him with a mouthful of grain in a bucket that you carry into the field, catch him, lead him through the gate, then let him have another mouthful in a second bucket outside the gate. After a few times, eliminate the bucket in the field but leave the bucket outside the gate. Eventually, you should be able to eliminate the outside bucket as well.

If this seems too elaborate, try to lure him with a bucket, catch and hold him for a few seconds, and then let him go. Do this repeatedly, so that he associates being caught only with receiving a little bribe. By the time you're ready to start bringing him in for work, he may have forgotten other associations.

As you are trying to convince him that being caught means good things, go out and catch him at feeding time, even if he can find his stall or feed bucket himself. Again, you want him to associate being caught with something positive.

HARD TO SHOE OR TRIM

Most unbroken horses don't receive as much attention from the farrier as working horses do, even when they have careful owners who make sure to keep up with trimming. Most of them are unshod, and they simply don't need their feet attended to every six or eight weeks. What's more, an unshod horse rarely needs his hooves cleaned out, since mud won't cake around the frog.

A horse turned out in suitable pasture may not even need much trimming if there's enough firmness in the ground to keep the wall short and enough moist areas to keep the horn soft and unbroken. An untrained horse may be unused to having his feet handled as much as they will have to be once he's shod.

If the problem is severe, consult a good farrier. He will tell you what kind of hobbles might be needed for safety. For a horse that's difficult rather than dangerous, following are some steps to take.

Pay attention to the lower legs as part of pleasant, low-stress grooming experiences. Brush and scratch him in a manner he likes, then brush down each leg. Don't ask him to pick up his feet until he's calm about being brushed down the leg as far as the coronet.

Once he accepts a thorough lower-leg brushing as part of his grooming, pick up the feet in the normal manner, using the same order each time. Brush a little more, doing nothing that might hurt or startle him. Don't hold the foot for long. Let him put it down as soon as he gets a little tense.

On the positive side, horses that have never been shod probably don't associate the farrier with pain. Their reluctance to have their feet handled is probably only an instinctive reluctance to be immobilized by having a foot in the air. Once they realize that it's not going to hurt, they should get over the problem.

EQUIPMENT

The unbroken adult horse will use the same kind of equipment in early training as a young horse. The equipment should be chosen carefully for any horse in training, regardless of his age, but extra care sometimes needs to be taken for an adult horse.

"I find that the older horses tend to be more sensitive to the equipment," Keffer-Nelson says. "It takes them longer to adjust to the bit, the saddle, the boots—to everything. They just need longer to get used to it and to accept it."

As a species, horses have acute tactile sensitivity—it's why they respond so well to a light tap of a whip—and that tendency has been allowed to develop to its ultimate level in an unused adult horse. They almost always react more actively than young horses to the kind of touching involved in training.

Some areas of equine skin are more sensitive than others. The head, neck, and shoulders are usually most responsive to the touch and most likely to be accidentally overstimulated. The horse may quickly become difficult to bridle if he has unpleasant experiences during bridle fitting.

To begin with, pick the bridle most likely to fit. Then, adjust the cheekstraps and noseband length as well as you can before placing it on the horse's head. Try not to put yourself and the horse in the position of fumbling with buckles while the bridle is in place, pinching and pulling his mouth and ears.

Be aware of where the reins are with the unbroken adult horse. What might be nothing more than a loose rein to a horse used to reins since babyhood may feel like a weapon striking the neck to an older, inexperienced one.

The top of the back isn't usually highly sensitive, but the thin skin covering the ribs and flanks is. Keep this in mind as you adjust pads and flaps of the saddle.

On the positive side, extra skin sensitivity helps a horse respond favorably to gentle pats on the neck. Scratching the withers helps calm an older horse as it does a young one. The older animals may even respond better, considering the stronger instinctive reaction to most stimuli.

Because of extra sensitivity and the fact that the skin hasn't developed any extra thickness where tack lies, be as careful as possible to pick equipment that's going to fit. You may find, as Keffer-Nelson did with Jhaelan, that even carefully fitted equipment can quickly change from well-fitted to not fitting at all.

"He outgrew several saddles during the first few months because he put on so much muscle in the back," she says. A mature horse in the prime of life doesn't grow in height, but he is inclined to develop strong new muscles quickly as a result of the new demands on his body.

Check the fit of all pieces of equipment regularly, and be prepared to make changes. If the equipment causes pain, the horse will learn that his work hurts rather than that he can do it and enjoy it.

BITS AND ADD-ONS

Bits used in the early training of an older horse are usually the same as for a young horse. "I start with a thick rubber snaffle, but not a flexible one," Keffer-Nelson says. "I then go on to a thick, heavy stainless-steel snaffle."

She uses heavier bits to start an older horse than she uses for a young one, but with both, she's likely to use a French mouth-training snaffle once the horse is carrying a rider.

Jhaelan, who is very strong in the head and neck, worked well with the loose center segment of the French mouth. "It gives him a little more to play with," she says, "so he's not stiff in his jaw. He's less resistant."

The flat linking piece in the center of the mouthpiece also serves to lessen the nutcracker effect on the sides of the mouth, making it a comfortable bit for a horse previously unused to a bit of any kind. It will help the horse remain soft-mouthed as he progresses in his training.

There are other training bits available, most of which are also designed to encourage the horse to mouth the bit and soften the jaw. Some of the mouthpieces have rollers, some have keys, and others have various links and loose sections. A training bit may be necessary to help discourage a strong-willed, strong-jawed adult horse that's thinking about seizing his bit and dashing away.

Some adult horses can be broken with a plain cavesson noseband attached to their bridle, but most mature horses are even more inclined than young horses to dream up ways to evade the bit by sliding it, getting the tongue over it, or otherwise misplacing it in the mouth. You may choose to begin very early with a dropped, flash, or figure-eight noseband to keep the mouth closed and the bit where it belongs. A horse that never gets into the habit of evading the bit will always be easier to handle.

Draw reins, side reins, and other head-setting devices are used on adult horses as well as on young ones as their training program progresses. Their overall independence and resistance often mean that these devices have to be introduced more slowly.

SADDLES

The saddle should be the best fitting, most comfortable saddle that you can find for the horse. Ideally, he will get his own saddle that can begin to mold to his back. Because of possible increased sensitivity, pay careful attention to pads and blankets, choosing absorbent materials that won't irritate skin that hasn't had anything rubbing against it for years. Pay very close attention to girths and cinches, making sure they don't pinch or irritate the skin. He won't like being girthed anyway, so there's no point in annoying him further by choosing a girth material that troubles him even more than the annoyance of confinement.

A light weight in the first saddle isn't as important for the fully grown horse as it is for the young one, since the horse has reached full development of his skeleton and soft tissues. More important than weight in the selection process is the choice of a saddle that distributes its weight and that of the rider over as large an area of the back as possible. The weight should be evenly distributed on both sides of the spinal column.

The even distribution of weight depends mostly on the quality of the saddle, but the weight-bearing area is a function of saddle design. Western and dressage saddles spread the weight over a wider area than forward-seat jumping saddles do. They may be a better choice for the initial months of training, even for a horse that you eventually hope to use in jumping.

Asking the horse to suddenly carry an additional 10 to 15 percent of his body weight over a small region around his shoulders will effect his firmly established center of balance and his free range of motion.

The broader distribution will have a less noticeable effect. Most adult horses that have never been ridden have steady gaits which you'll want to refine rather than rediscover after they've been damaged.

The choice for Jhaelan turned out to be a synthetic dressage saddle, which was light and flexible, to help his sensitive back. Both Western and English saddles of various designs are available in synthetic materials. All are light in comparison to their leather equivalents, and most tend to mold to a horse's back.

Whether you choose leather or synthetic, the saddle should fit, should be rechecked for fit regularly, and should be placed on enough padding to cushion the vulnerable areas of the horse's shoulder and back.

OTHER EQUIPMENT

Most horses new to training need protective equipment. "I use full wraps even though the older horses tend to be sounder," Keffer-Nelson says. More specialized boots may also be necessary, depending on the demands of his lungeing or work under a rider.

Older horses are often secure in their footing and smooth in their gaits, and some may be less likely than young ones to brush and interfere. But leg and foot injuries early in a training program can be so damaging to a horse's psychological development and his attitude towards work that it's almost always best to take precautions. This is particularly true if the horse is put through the kind of extensive ground training on the lunge and long reins that the older untrained horse usually needs to make him safe to train under saddle.

CONDITIONING

The amount of pretraining conditioning needed by an adult horse depends on his living circumstances during his idle years. If he's been stalled and otherwise treated like a horse that gets exercise during work, he probably needs exercise even before preliminary training begins. He may be overweight, but even if he isn't, his muscles may not be up to the stresses of training.

*A horse will give himself some exercise
when turned out. Some keep themselves
in good working condition.*

"If an older horse hasn't had any work or conditioning, I would start by turning him out every day for as long as you can manage," Keffer-Nelson says. "Turn him out with other horses if possible."

Horses in average domestic circumstances don't usually keep themselves superbly fit, but they can get reasonable exercise for their muscles and bones as well as some aerobic conditioning if they are kept moving by their own personalities or by other horses. Try several weeks of turnout before moving to the next step of conditioning.

Handling remains important even with a turned-out horse, because ground training will require catching, leading, standing for equipment, and other handling by humans before work actually begins. Untrained horses that have otherwise been treated like other adult horses may be easy to handle. If not, you will have to spend hours or days teaching handling manners, preferably while the horse is still receiving exercise at pasture.

The horse then moves to the ring. "I would start with some free lungeing, preferably in a small ring, using a whip," Keffer-Nelson says. "This is more conditioning than training, although you're asking him to walk, trot, canter, and listen to the halt commands. It's nothing too formal, just enough to give him some good exercise about twenty minutes a day."

A previously untrained adult horse will probably already know some voice commands just from being around handlers who use them. He's likely to have been told "Whoa" by a farrier who wanted him to

Some unbroken adult horses need basic training in manners while being handled.

stand still, or "Stop" by someone trying to prevent him from rushing into a stall. Although the mature horse may not want to start paying extra attention to human beings, his already acute sense of hearing will permit him to learn more voice commands and to learn them quickly.

Sound is extremely important to horses, as you'll realize by watching a horse's ears for thirty seconds. Between them, they're designed to pick up sounds from a complete circle around his body. The long neck helps him move those ears into even more appropriate locations to hear and locate the origin of the sounds.

As an animal that's learned over years to rely on himself and other horses for stimulation and, he thinks, protection, the untrained mature horse is probably even more aware of and responsive to sounds than a younger one. The nervous adult horse can be reassured, the naughty one scolded, and the untrained one introduced to new words and sounds very effectively.

The early days of free lungeing should be used to teach or reinforce the halt command of "Whoa" or "Halt" (one or the other, not both). The horse can also begin to learn "Walk on" or "Forward."

This period of free lungeing is usually done with a regular halter, not the full lungeing equipment needed for proper control. "Don't even use a chain unless you're being dragged all over the place," Keffer-Nelson says. "The whip is usually just to keep him away from you."

The length of time required for free lungeing depends on the level of conditioning the horse has reached, as well as his attitude towards the entire process. If you are used to working with young horses, you may be surprised by the length of time it takes to get the older unbroken horse ready for serious training.

"An older horse almost always needs more ground work than a young horse," Keffer-Nelson says. "I want to be absolutely sure he knows his voice commands in addition to being physically ready. I find that the older horses are more resistant. The young ones seem to be more surprised by the whole process, while the older ones may be combative."

LEARNING TO CROSSTIE

Many adult horses, even if unbroken to ride, were taught to crosstie early in their lives. That will be a great advantage now, since equipment is much easier to fit and fasten to a horse that's willing to stand while tied.

It's not impossible to tack a horse that won't crosstie, but it requires an assistant, a stall or other small enclosed space, and time and patience. Horses are much easier to teach to crosstie when they're young, but it can be done with an older horse too.

"Training an older horse to tie can be difficult since he's so big," Keffer-Nelson says. "They can be dangerous both because of size and because they usually don't feel any need to please people. I'd approach it the same way I do with young horses, but with extra care."

Being tied is not a comfortable situation for any horse, but the mature horse that's spent years not having to tolerate it will find the concept more uncomfortable than any other horse. In the wild, the horse's first line of defense from predators is flight. Being tied prevents that, and the instincts of even the most domesticated horse tell him not to permit himself to be restrained—something deep in his being tells him that death may result.

Sensible horse keepers will start handling a foal from the day he is born, teaching him to lead with a halter by asking him to walk alongside his mother. Being led this way to standing with his mother while she's tied to being tied himself are natural steps for him.

A horse that has long forgotten his mother and hasn't been restrained by something more stationary than a human being holding a lead rope will probably be frightened and may rebel during tying. Following is the procedure Janet Keffer-Nelson uses.

"I put a big, soft cotton rope around the heart girth," she says. "Then it goes through the front legs, up the chest, and through the halter ring.

"The rope continues up above the head, maybe seven feet off the ground, where I'll tie it to something sturdy with a quick-release knot.

I leave a very long tail so I can hold the end of the rope, but well out of the horse's way."

The advantage of this method, she says, is that it avoids injury to the neck. The danger of neck injury is not as great to an older horse as to a young one, but it's still something to be avoided.

"The good thing about this procedure is that when the horse panics and falls back, the pull comes from behind his shoulders," she says. "He's pulled forward, and when he continues to move forward, the rope loosens around him. You're not risking injury to his neck behind the poll, because he's not really being pulled from his halter."

Even this procedure is likely to prompt rebellion in mature, unbroken horses. They have many years of enjoying independence to overcome, and it's unlikely to be done quickly. Keffer-Nelson says she sometimes works on tie training after the horse has been heavily exercised.

"It's a safety factor," she says. "With the older horses, I'll try it when he's tired and seems more amenable."

TRAINING

Proper training of a young horse almost always begins with formal lungeing, mostly because it's the least stressful way to introduce control, steady gaits, and obedience. It's also valuable because most people want to begin training before the horse is entirely ready to carry the weight of a rider.

With the adult horse, you don't have to worry about him being physically ready to carry the rider, but you certainly have to be concerned about him being psychologically ready. Preparation prior to mounting is important both because you want the horse to have positive experiences early in his training and because a mature horse unready for a rider can be extremely dangerous.

Ground training is much safer than mounted training. It provides the forum you'll need to create the respectful relationship that any horse has to develop with his trainer before he will allow himself to be made usable.

Respect is the key word. "There's a fine line in training between fear and respect," Keffer-Nelson says. "I want my horse to be a little afraid of me so that I know he's going to respect my wishes. I want him to know that when I ask him to do something, I expect an immediate response."

But a little fear doesn't mean terror. A horse shouldn't think that he is going to be injured, but he should think he doesn't have any alternative but to obey. That means firmness and determination, but no violent responses to any rebellion.

Rebellion will almost certainly come.

"The older horses tend to be more strong-willed," Keffer-Nelson says. "It's harder for them to develop a respect for people. Youngsters seem to develop it quickly. You're bigger than they are, and they know it."

Or, at least, the young horse *suspects* that the human being might be bigger than he is. The adult horse knows perfectly well that he's bigger and stronger than the human being.

The horse can enter the ring for serious training with a lungeing cavesson or his regular halter. With the former, the lunge rein snaps or buckles to the top of the noseband, while with the latter, the rein

Expect defiance and occasional rebellion from an adult unbroken horse.

attaches to the halter ring on the bottom. The lungeing cavesson permits greater control of the horse's head during the procedure, but work on pace, gaits, and voice commands can be done with a regular halter.

The early lessons should be done with at least two people, one at the end of the lunge rein and the other at or near the horse's head to help direct and control him. A well-behaved horse can dispense with the helper at the head quickly, but a rebellious one will need a helper nearby for most of the early lessons.

As with the young horse, the older horse can be moved from lungeing in a cavesson or halter to lungeing in a bitted bridle. The steps followed with the older horse may take a little longer than they would with a young one, but progress should be steady.

Each time a new piece of equipment is introduced, do it gradually, perhaps after completing a lesson. Attach it, leave it on the horse for a few seconds or minutes, then take it off and put the horse away.

The introduction of the surcingle will be critical, since it's so much like the girth that he's later going to have to accept. When he's feeling relaxed, perhaps after eating or being groomed, try laying something over the horse's back. It should be something soft that can't hurt him, perhaps a towel at first, then maybe something a little heavier like a stirrup leather complete with stirrup.

Well-cared-for horses may have worn a blanket with a surcingle strap, and they may need only a brief introduction to a strap around the middle not sewed into a blanket. Others should be handled more carefully, with the surcingle laid over the back but not attached, then loosely attached, then firmly buckled. These lessons can take place after the halter-lungeing lessons and should be of very short duration if the horse seems restive.

Eventually, the horse should tolerate the surcingle at its normal tightness. Try a few lungeing lessons with the surcingle properly tightened but not attached to draw reins or long reins. Given his tactile sensitivity, permit the horse to adjust to the feeling of a snug strap around his belly before he has to get used to the feel of an additional rein.

Long reining the horse teaches him to obey simple rein signals and to obey his human handler.

As with the young horse, once the horse is lungeing in good control and good balance with side reins, he can be worked with long reins, which more nearly simulate the kind of rein signals he will get as a ridden horse. The older horse will probably be more nervous with a human being directly behind him than a young one, so make sure he can see and hear you working at his side before trying to move directly behind him. His well-established instincts will make him more inclined than the young horse to confuse the trainer with a predator.

The introduction of the saddle will probably not be much of a problem for a horse that's used to a surcingle, but care needs to be taken anyway. Let the horse see and smell the saddle. Consider leaving it within his sight for several hours as he lounges comfortably in his stall. The first time you put it on his back, take off the leathers, stirrups, and girth and just lay it on his back for a few seconds. Increase the time gradually, add the leathers and stirrups, and then the girth. Finally, fasten the girth loosely and walk the horse around.

Once the horse accepts the presence of the saddle, he may be lunged or long reined in it, first with stirrups run up the leathers, then with them down but tied in place, then with them loose. The loose stirrup may cause the greatest single equine upset in the entire process.

Only after the horse willingly accepts the saddle and its annoyances do you consider mounting the horse. Although mounting should be a natural progression from the previous steps of training—and is accepted as such by many young horses—it's a more difficult and dangerous procedure with many older animals.

"Mature strength and size can be a problem," Keffer-Nelson says. "Older horses realize that they've never been asked to do this before. They wonder why they're being asked now."

The first person to mount the horse should be a good rider who's agile enough to dismount quickly should danger develop. As with young horses, the steps, from putting a little human weight on the back

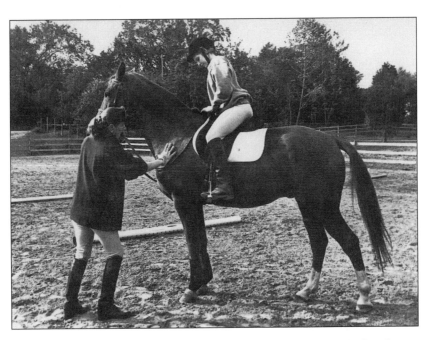

First mounting requires two people and extreme sensitivity to the horse's tension and nervousness.

to putting a foot in the stirrup to climbing aboard, should be steady and slow.

Always work with one or more assistants for the first several lessons, at least until the horse has completed several lessons in a row without attempting to unseat the rider. Older horses as well as young ones often need a halter in addition to their bridle so the assistant can quickly take hold of the horse if he misbehaves.

While it's generally best not to ask the horse to move faster until he is quite secure at the previous pace, that's not necessarily true in the step between standing still and walking forward. Horses, particularly older ones, tend to look at being required to stand still as being confined. They are often less nervous and tense when walking, and they should be permitted to walk almost immediately. Moving faster than a walk, however, should be delayed until the horse is secure and calm at the walk.

Within a few weeks, the horse should be able to trot calmly, and the lessons can include brief periods of the faster gait. But cantering usually has to be delayed for quite a while, even months, with the older unbroken horse. The canter is exciting to most horses, and a green animal that seems calm at the walk and trot may quickly revert to being uncontrollable at the canter. Don't ask for anything faster than a trot until the horse is controllable in his pace, his forward movement, and his reaction to aids at the slower gaits.

More advanced training proceeds in the same way that it does with younger horses. Many short sessions are preferable to a few long ones during the early months, but the adult horse should be physically ready for long work sessions sooner than the very young horse is. He will have to learn to accept the bit, move forward straight from the leg, and understand both rein and leg aids. After he has fully adjusted to his new career as a horse in work, he will probably progress at about the same pace as a younger horse.

It can be a challenge to get an adult horse to that point. But if you do, your success will bring both great satisfaction and a usable animal.

CHAPTER TWELVE

The Long Unused Horse

UNLIKE THE UNBROKEN ADULT HORSE, THE long unused horse may have been very well trained at one point in his life. But he hasn't been asked to work in a long time, and he may need help before he can be useful again. Understanding the reason for his idleness is the first step in his retraining program.

Horses remain unused for extended periods for many of the same reasons that other horses aren't broken in the first place. An owner's lack of time or inclination to ride is probably the most common reason. Outgrown horses and ponies, and animals left behind when a child goes off to college fit into this category. A horse in this situation will probably need conditioning, a hoof and health tune-up, and a few refresher lessons.

A horse that turned out not to be quite what a new owner expected may also have been left unused. The owner may have wanted to use him in a different sport from the one in which he was trained, and the horse didn't receive the lessons that would have converted him to his new activity. This horse will need the same things mentioned above, but he will also need some retraining for his new sport. After you've completed the steps in this chapter, consult the chapter that corresponds to your horse's new sport for information on how to retrain him.

A horse may be unused because he was more difficult or more poorly trained than a buyer expected. A horse that was very poorly trained might best be considered an unbroken adult horse. In this situation, consult Chapter Eleven.

Finally, a horse may be coming off a breeding farm where he wasn't ridden or driven for years. Most mares, if they were well broken in the first place, need only conditioning and a few easy lessons to return to usefulness. Some mares—and many more stallions—need a greater number of lessons. A stallion may also need castration if he is extremely difficult to handle and keep.

In the case of each horse that was once broken, you have equine instincts to deal with. As with the unbroken adult horse, the instincts have had a chance to reestablish themselves strongly. But in the case of one vital instinct, its strength can be a great advantage as you return the horse to training.

MEMORY

The horse has evolved, over fifty million years, from the cat-sized Eohippus into the animal we know today. The species has changed enormously over the millennia, but virtually none of the change is a result of human interference.

It's true that selective breeding has created horses that are bigger or smaller than average, horses stronger or faster than most, and horses of colors that appeal to human beings. But the characteristics that make a horse a horse exist because the ancestors of the modern horse needed them to live, not because people thought that they were nice things to have in their most useful companion animal.

Perhaps the most important of these characteristics is the fabled equine memory. That memory is what enables us to train horses in the first place, and it's what allows us to not use a horse for years, then saddle him up and ride away.

But a horse's exceptional memory doesn't exist because it makes him more trainable—it exists so that he can remember where in his range of thousands of acres he can find water in a dry summer, new grass in a late spring, and shelter in a snowy winter. He can remember all of those things, even if he saw them only once ten years ago.

He needs to remember where the predators hang out so that he doesn't seek shelter in the same rocky cave where a lion once leaped on a herdmate. It doesn't matter that the domestic horse has water delivered into his tank, feed placed in his tub, and lions excluded from his pasture. He still knows how to remember.

All animals have to feed and protect themselves, so memory plays a part in all of their lives at some level. But horses in particular are in need of self-protection, having few weapons, a long gestation period and a comparatively long period of infancy, and a requirement for vast quantities of food every day.

So they remember. The ability to remember has survived domestication, but to the horse, its purpose hasn't changed a bit. To take advantage of the horse's memory while training or retraining, keep in mind that it doesn't exist so he can remember how to do what people want.

In returning a previously trained horse to service, you make use of the horse's prodigious memory while realizing that the horse's ability to learn and remember has evolved differently from that of humans for practical reasons. Horses remember best things that serve to protect them.

They can learn other things, too, but most horses remember some things they learn far better than they do others. Some aspects of their early training may be forgotten, while others are with them forever.

Because of their overriding concern for self-preservation, horses remember best the things that they learn are safe. Activities and places that they've become used to are remembered as safe and will usually be accepted throughout their lives. This type of learning is usually called habituation, and some scientists believe that it's the most temporary kind of learning. Maybe so, but it's very easily used in returning a horse to work. In the real world of retraining, it means that a horse that was accustomed to performing in a particular place or manner, even years ago, will quite easily become accustomed to it again. If the horse was yours when he used to be worked, reintroduce him to working by placing him in the same ring, on the same trails, with the same rider, if possible. He will be reaccustomed to work without having to go through the process of discovering that no monsters are waiting in the corner of the ring or at the next turn in the trail.

If he wasn't yours, try to find out as much as you can about his working circumstances and simulate, as well as you can, his previous working conditions. This is necessary only at first. Once the horse becomes comfortable with work again, he can be introduced to new circumstances as can any adult horse.

Horses are also good at retaining latent memories. This is important to a horse that needs to remember where a watering hole is even though he trotted past it only once three years ago and wasn't looking for water at the time. The horse's latent memory is difficult for most human beings to understand, since we don't always share the talent for it. We often don't remember things unless we're interested in them at the time we see them.

A latent memory is what sometimes spooks a horse when there's nothing spooky around or makes him refuse a jump when every other jump—identical to our eyes—is no problem for him. When returning a horse to training, you may find his latent memories interfering with normal progression. Since you probably don't share the memories, the only thing you can do is to habituate him to whatever it is that he remembers.

Repeated exposure is the solution. If something at a jump disturbs him, for example, let him see the jump, smell the jump, and walk or trot over a smaller version of it. Eventually he should accept it.

The foundation for most horse training is another kind of training—the conditioned response. It worked with Pavlov's dogs, and it works with horses. The horse returning to work will remember skills learned with the conditioned response provided no other responses have been superimposed during the period that he was out of action.

In the conditioned response, the horse learns that every time he feels or hears a particular cue, he's supposed to supply a particular response. In the early days of training, the conditioned response works hand-in-hand with the so-called Skinnerian method, in which the horse performs an action to avoid punishment. A pull back on the reins is a cue to stop or slow. When he does, the pressure lessens. If he hears the word "Whoa" or "Halt" at the same time that he feels the pressure, he will become conditioned to stop on that word with no punishment-avoidance involved.

During his years of inactivity, handlers may have used the word "Whoa" to prevent him from rushing into his stall for his dinner. Once he's under a rider again, the response to stop may no longer be there, since he will be reconditioned to avoid rushing to his feed on that cue. In reality, horses rarely forget the meaning of the word "Whoa," but it's a simplified example of how conditioned responses can be altered over years of disuse.

Retraining for these horses may require a careful, step-by-step return to most of the skills the horse used to know. More on that later. But before retraining begins, the long unused horse needs some practical attention.

HEALTH CARE

Unused horses vary in how well they have been cared for while out of training, depending on the owner and the reasons they've been unused. Some are treated exactly like every other horse in the barn and will need no special attention before being put through conditioning and then a retraining program. Others will need more care.

VACCINATIONS

It's tempting to neglect vaccinations for a horse that is not being used. Whether it's because you figure he isn't going anywhere and won't be catching any stray germs or because you tend to forget about all but his most basic needs, many horses that are not being trained or ridden are behind in their vaccinations.

Updating vaccinations has a dual purpose. It will protect him as he becomes more active, of course. But it also provides an opportunity to have a veterinarian give him a quick checkup to assess his overall health. If you're willing to pay, you can have a complete examination done, including laboratory work and a thorough soundness check. But even if you want to keep expenses low, a brief examination by a vet as he or she vaccinates can be a useful tool in determining how hard the horse can work and how much conditioning he needs.

All horses need certain vaccinations to protect them from those diseases that are usually fatal. They all need a tetanus vaccination, and most need vaccination against one or more of the forms of equine encephalitis. In most parts of North America, they need a rabies vaccination. In a few areas, a Potomac Horse Fever vaccination is advisable.

Other vaccines depend on the age of the horse, the use you intend for him, and how often he's in contact with other horses. These vaccines, mostly for respiratory diseases, are useful for horses shipped to shows, group trail rides, and other activities away from home. They may be particularly important with animals that have had little contact with other horses for a number of years, since they won't have as much natural immunity. The first few times at group events also create stress, which makes them more vulnerable to disease. Consult your veterinarian about what's appropriate for the horse.

In addition, ask for a Coggins test if you plan to transport your horse to shows or other activities. The test, to identify antibodies for Equine Infectious Anemia in the bloodstream, is required by most shows. The horse won't be allowed on the grounds unless he has a current negative Coggins report.

The form is also necessary for interstate shipping. The test results take a couple of weeks to come back from the lab, so you should have plenty of time if you have the horse checked as you begin retraining him.

DENTAL CARE

A long unused horse may have also had his teeth neglected. Equine teeth don't decay as often as human teeth do, but they do develop a host of other problems. A horse out of training may not show the loss of condition that a working horse does when his teeth need work, so problems may have developed unnoticed by even a conscientious owner.

Most common are uneven wear and the development of sharp edges on the molars. Uneven edges prevent the teeth from grinding the food properly, and they can also irritate the soft tissue of the mouth and tongue. Once the bit is added to the equation, the discomfort may become intense. You'll probably need a veterinarian or equine dentist to float the teeth—to file the uneven edges so that the teeth can meet properly.

Other problems include unnecessary extra teeth, often wolf teeth, that should be removed to prevent bit interference. You may find that behavioral problems that left the horse unused were due to mouth difficulties that prevented him from accepting the bit.

Remember to reexamine the mouth periodically during training, especially if the horse seems to be having difficulty with the bit. He may have a mouth or tooth shape that makes one bit more uncomfortable than another. A bit that causes discomfort in itself usually identifies itself with tissue irritation in the mouth.

LATE CASTRATION

Most male horses are gelded as yearlings or two-year-olds. Those whose owners have ambitions to breed them, and those whose owners never got around to it, are left intact to develop stallions' secondary sex characteristics and behavior patterns.

A horse can be castrated at any age, but if it's done after the age of three or four, the stallion-like appearance isn't going to disappear. A horse will retain the crested neck of a stallion, and his bones will be heavier than the bones of mares or horses gelded before maturity.

His personality will probably improve; although he will probably show somewhat more "studdish" behavior than he would if he had been gelded as a young horse. Still, you should find him easier to handle, more inclined to remember what he's taught, and able to be turned out with other horses without attacking or trying to breed with them.

The surgery is slightly more dangerous and requires a little more advanced planning than it does with a young horse. Potential danger exists for both the horse and the vet. The blood vessels in the scrotal region are a little larger in a fully adult horse, increasing the danger of bleeding. The adult horse's size and weight will also increase the amount of anesthesia required, bringing a danger of its own.

His larger size also increases the danger to the person performing the surgery. The operation can be performed with the horse standing— it's the quickest and usually safest for the horse—but the adult animal's height and strength may make it more likely that he can kick or strike out against the vet.

Most vets choose to operate on the adult horse while he's lying down under general anesthesia, but this method requires more anesthesia, more time (in which the animal can be injured), and more difficulty in getting the horse safely up. The choice is usually up to the person performing the surgery.

With an adult horse as well as a young one, recovery from castration should be quick, provided the incision is allowed to drain properly, with moderate exercise immediately after recovery from anesthesia. Even a fully vaccinated horse is usually given a tetanus booster before or after the surgery. This is vital if a horse hasn't been kept up with his vaccinations.

Ridgelings, also called cryptorchids, require special consideration. These male horses have one undescended testicle, reducing their fertility, but usually not their stallion-like appearance and personality. Castration of ridgelings is more difficult than normal gelding operations, depending on the extent of the problem, and may require hospitalization.

HOOF CARE

Horses out of training for extended periods almost always need special attention paid to their feet. Their hooves may be in excellent condition if they have been turned out unshod in large pastures with other horses and if they've had at least occasional trimming.

But horses don't always wear their feet evenly, and a horse with uneven hooves may have caused damage to both his feet and his sense of balance. Moreover, because minor lameness is seldom noticed in an unused horse, he may have had foot injuries that weren't treated.

First, examine the horse's feet and hooves yourself. If the horse hasn't been asked to pick up his feet in some time, he may be reluctant.

Consult Chapter Eleven for information on accustoming an older horse to hoof examination. Provided he once knew how to do it, it should only take a few minutes to induce him to pick up his feet.

Look for cracks and chips on the edge of the hoof wall. The horse may have dry hooves that need dressing, or he may just need a trimming. If little cracks cover the entire hoof wall, he may need extra dressing and perhaps a change in his diet.

Uneven wear around the rim of the hoof usually means that he's been untrimmed too long. But it may also indicate unsoundness, with the horse putting pressure on one side of the foot rather than evenly across its entire surface.

Conversely, hooves that have worn down evenly but too much don't adequately protect the soles, which can become bruised or irritated. The frog, too, can be damaged by overworn hoof walls. Horses with too-short hoof walls will probably need treatment before any kind of training can begin.

A horse whose hoof appears to have worn evenly with sufficient wall to protect the inner structures, whose frog is flexible and clean, and whose sole is unbruised can begin conditioning without trimming or shoeing. One with any hoof problems should be examined by a farrier, vet, or both for suggestions on trimming, treatment, or padding.

As training progresses, the horse will need regular trimming, at least enough to assure even wear. He will probably need to be shod, unless you plan to use him only occasionally and only on soft surfaces.

THE RETRAINING PROGRAMS

The program you follow depends on the level of training that the horse reached earlier in his life. Also important is his current age and condition. Whatever his category, he's going to need some work before he's expected to learn (or relearn) skills.

THE OVERFED, UNDEREXERCISED HORSE

Some idle horses are fed exactly the same as other, working horses in the barn. Their hay is the same, their grain is the same, and their pasture turnout is the same. The difference comes in the exercise that the horse gets. In the case of the unused horse, it's usually next to nothing.

Like people, some horses gain weight on this kind of program. They make themselves obvious to even the most unobservant owner, and they may actually have been placed on a diet even before being returned to work. If your horse has not been placed on a diet, then do it now. In order to prevent unhappiness and discomfort, try reducing his grain ration while maintaining or increasing his hay allotment. Alternately, choose a grain or pellet that provides fewer calories.

The overfed and underexercised horse most likely to cause problems during his return to training is the one that hasn't gained weight from his owner's generosity. Instead, he's gained energy and high spirits.

Before either training or formal conditioning, turn the horse out for as many hours a day as you can, in the company of as many horses as

A long unused horse can burn off energy and begin conditioning himself by being turned out with other horses.

you can locate. He will exercise himself and take the edge off some of his excessive energy. He probably won't get himself into the kind of condition he will need to work, but it will help both his attitude and his physique.

At the same time, make sure that he's getting the kind of feed that he needs. If he hasn't gained weight on his previous diet, he doesn't need fewer calories. But he may need a lower protein feed, less grain and more hay, or a different balance in his feeding program.

Next, put the horse on a lungeing program. He will gain physical conditioning and mental discipline in a manner that's safer for the trainer than hopping aboard. He needs to return his mind and body to the world of work in a manner that won't permit him to throw a rider or otherwise misbehave in dangerous ways. Not only do you not want to be injured, but it's not good for his progress in retraining for him to be dumping riders.

How long he has to be lunged depends on how well he accepts the process and how much exercise he's able to receive. A horse well trained earlier in his life will probably become reaccustomed to lungeing quickly and will rapidly improve both in his willingness to work on the line and the benefits he receives.

A horse that was poorly or quickly trained while young will probably not progress so rapidly. You may need to treat the horse as almost unbroken and follow the procedure outlined in Chapter Eleven. It's wise to do this so that he does learn to lunge well, even if you're tempted to skip lungeing altogether and move directly to mounted retraining. The exercise will be balanced, controlled, and ideal for both the physical and mental discipline needed for a horse that is being returned to service after years of idleness.

When his physical condition is improved and he has become easier to handle, you may move on to riding. Your first ride should be similar to those used to test the knowledge of a horse being converted from Western to English, or vice versa. Consult Chapters Four and Five.

If the horse was previously used by you or someone you know, you are probably familiar with his skills. During the first ride, you are checking for how well he remembers them. With a less familiar horse, you want to know what he learned and what he remembers from his working life.

Start at the beginning, with start, stop, and steering. Even a minimally broken horse will probably remember the cues and you may immediately move to more difficult commands. Add the leg cues to turn, to back, to move to faster gaits, and to strike off on the correct lead at the canter. The horse may resist any or all of the commands, but you should persist until he responds correctly.

Try to progress naturally, as you would with an unbroken horse. This gives him a chance to adjust his mind and body to the new requests as they are given him. Random requests will be difficult for a horse that hasn't responded to cues for years.

The first ride should be fairly brief, since you want it to be a positive experience and you don't want the horse to be stressed or overwhelmed by difficult demands early in his retraining. It's important that he has positive thoughts of the process.

After completing your first ride, decide where the problem areas are. The horse may do fine in the early steps, knowing how to start, halt, turn, and transition to faster gaits smoothly. He may be a little less secure on lead changes. Find the point just before the problems appear, and begin to work at that point.

You will go through the skills one by one as you would with a young horse, but you will almost certainly find that the previously trained horse will progress very rapidly. Just remember that, during the early days of retraining, his physical condition will probably be less good than it was when he was fully active. He may be mentally ready to do lateral movements again, but his legs, chest, and hindquarters may not be prepared for the stress of them.

Long unused horses sometimes have nasty habits that they either developed or perfected during their period of idleness. Those with too much energy sometimes refuse to maintain a steady pace at the slower gaits. When they should be walking slowly, they add a little running step. When they should be trotting evenly, they alternate long strides with short ones, adding the occasional canter stride into the mix.

Collect the horse slightly when he adds his extra strides, keep good contact with the reins, and urge him steadily but not too strongly with the leg. Trotting poles on the lunge line or mounted are useful, too.

Horses out of training sometimes come back as pullers, even though they didn't pull earlier in their lives. It may be a result of the fact that they have had their own way for years and they now choose to have their own way in terms of speed and pace.

Before changing to a more severe bit, try to control pulling by collecting the horse with a slight, forgiving rein pull every time he pulls against the bit. Follow this half halt with an urge to move forward. If he persists in pulling, try alternating forward movement with turns so that both you and he can relax your grips. Try to avoid making it a battle of strength between you and the horse. That's a battle that the horse invariably wins.

More dangerous is the horse that bucks. The previously trained horse that bucks may resent having to work again and feels good enough to try to eliminate work by eliminating his rider. Keeping the horse's head up and his body moving strongly forward prevents him from getting into the proper posture for bucking. If your sport requires a lower head and a leisurely gait, worry about this after he's gotten over his tendency to buck.

More common, and nearly as dangerous, is the horse that rears. Keeping his head up won't help here. In fact, a horse that rears may need a dropped noseband, martingale, or some other device to keep him from raising his head too high. If the horse tries to rear, ride him strongly forward with leg cues and even the whip. In following the cues, he won't be able to rear.

THE OLDER UNUSED HORSE

Many horses have been out of action for years because they have been retired, officially or effectively, from their original work. They may be broodmares, old horses, or horses that were retired from sports because of injury. Some may fit into the other category of overfed and underexercised, but in this section we'll discuss those whose energy level may be a little lower.

If the horse was unused because of a previous injury, have him checked before asking him to do anything more than light conditioning on a lunge line. A healthy middle-aged horse can begin work immediately, light at first, as can most elderly ones. The very old horse should normally not be asked to progress to anything more than walking and slow trotting under a rider until you're sure he can handle more.

The older unused horse should be turned out as much as possible in the weeks leading up to his retraining. He will gain some condition outside, although not nearly enough to return to use. His feed should also be assessed. He may need a higher-calorie feed to provide energy for his new work, but he will probably not need a higher level of protein, at least until his workload becomes substantial.

What he will need is conditioning. The first step for a horse that is badly out of condition will be to lead him with a halter and lead rope. This will also reaccustom him to being handled.

*Simple walking with halter and lead helps condition
badly out-of-shape old horses.*

You can lunge the older horse to help condition him, but his energy level will probably be such that you can safely return him to condition under a rider. On your first ride, do a simple test of his ability to start, stop, and turn, then ride very slowly for the length of the lesson. This will probably be no more than fifteen or twenty minutes, less if the horse seems badly out of condition.

Add a minute or two each day—an everyday workout is not too much if you stick to a walk—until the horse is comfortable working for half an hour at the walk. Then add a minute or so at the trot, slowly increasing the percentage of trotting in the half-hour lesson.

Depending on the horse's condition and age, you may canter briefly after several weeks of easier work. Once the horse can handle each of the gaits, check the other skills that the horse used to have, including lead changes, lateral moves, collection, head carriage, and anything else appropriate to your sport.

As with the more energetic unused horse, checking skills in the order that they were taught will seem familiar to the horse and will most likely cause less stress. Throughout the retraining process, be careful not to ask too much too soon of the older horse. It's not mental stress that you need to be concerned about, but rather physical stress and injury.

Older horses develop well with long, slow workouts. Most of the training sessions should consist of walking, slow trotting, and only brief periods of more intensive training in skills. Once the horse returns to good condition, you can ask for a more demanding physical performance.

Occasionally, your intentionally slow progress will help a horse decide to take advantage of you. With normal equine stubbornness honed during their years of freedom, they may become unwilling to go in particular directions or walk past certain points. Some become barn rats, unwilling to leave the barn or saddling enclosure to go out and work. Whipping and kicking will solve the problem temporarily, but it does nothing to improve a horse's willingness to work.

Persistent, nonviolent urging is necessary with these horses, as are a few tricks. Horses dislike the feeling of being off balance, so directing a

Long, slow, low-pressure workouts provide the best conditioning for the long unused old horse.

stubborn and stationary horse in a tight circle will usually get him moving. After a few circles, he may be willing to move out under normal urging. You may have to repeat this procedure several times during each workout, but after a few times of being forced or tricked into moving out and forward, the horse should give up this particular bad habit.

By nature, horses are physically active creatures that like to move their bodies. Nature requires them to move when they live in the wild. Otherwise, they couldn't feed and protect themselves. But some horses do become lazy, and the older, long-unused horse is a good candidate for this.

At its most benign, laziness in a horse is simply annoying. The horse won't work as quickly or as energetically as you want, and you have to constantly urge him to do more. It can be dangerous when it leads to stumbling or repeated missteps.

Make sure that the horse isn't being lazy because he is in pain, uncomfortable, or otherwise impaired. Then work on changing the physical and mental attitude that leads to laziness. Some horses respond well to the simple knowledge that you have a whip. Let him see it and let him feel it, gently, when you want him to act more lively.

But you don't want to have to whack your horse every time you expect him to move actively, so you should try to make alertness part of his normal movement. Ask him for things that force him to pay attention. Try repeated turns, serpentines, and figure eights. Keep him on the bit and moving forward, perhaps with his head a little higher or a little lower than he chooses. Talk to him, and make your voice part of his urging to keep moving.

Don't make him work beyond his capabilities. An old horse can concentrate longer than a young one, but he may not have the physical ability to keep his muscles tuned for as long as you might expect. Keep his workouts brief until he's back in shape, but keep him alert during the entire time under saddle.

A horse that was once well trained can be returned to work fairly rapidly, but you should realize that he may never reach the skill level that he attained earlier in his life. The older horse may not have the physical capacity to do what he did before. The middle-aged one may be so firmly established in the physical patterns of idleness that he has overridden forever the balance and movement he needs in his sport.

But, in the absence of active injury, both horses should be able to come close to what they used to be able to do. Their maturity may actually make them better overall performers and certainly better companions than they were in their younger days.

Index